Preparatory Reports
SECOND VATICAN COUNCIL

Preparatory Reports
SECOND
VATICAN COUNCIL

Translated by
ARAM BERARD, S.J.

THE WESTMINSTER PRESS
PHILADELPHIA

Imprimi potest: John V. O'Connor, S.J., Provincial, New England Province

Nihil obstat: Rt. Rev. Matthew P. Stapleton, Diocesan Censor

Imprimatur: ✠ Richard Cardinal Cushing, Archbishop of Boston

JULY 9, 1965

LIBRARY OF CONGRESS CATALOG CARD No. 65–19280

To Dad

*in gratitude
especially for our
many discussions
together*

Published by The Westminster Press®
Philadelphia, Pennsylvania

PRINTED IN THE UNITED STATES OF AMERICA

BX
830
1962
A3
B4

CONTENTS

8 CONTENTS

FOREWORD

PREPARATORY REPORTS — SECOND VATICAN COUNCIL renders available in English a valuable and indispensable source for future historians of the Council. If the phenomenon of vital growth from seed to perfect maturity presents baffling problems in the order of natural science, it should not be surprising that the interventions of God in salvation history are ineffably more mysterious. Despite its official title, " The Second Vatican Council," this extraordinary manifestation of the Spirit aimed at the revitalization of Christianity will go down in history as the Johannine Council, the legacy and heritage of Pope John XXIII.

The providential crises of this century, including two world wars, the menace of enslaving totalitarian regimes, the end of colonialism and the sudden appearance of entirely new nations, rapid advances in technology, the economic interdependence of all men, the struggles of the cold war, the ominous threat of a nuclear holocaust — all these and other factors have done much to break down the narrow prejudices of entrenched cultures, and to bring home to men's hearts the fact that they are all members of one family. It is in this climate of radical change, of which Pope John was so vitally conscious, that he was inspired to inaugurate the Second Vatican Council: " All signs point out that our Lord himself, with the grace of his Holy Spirit, has inspired this salutary project; the very idea of calling the Council was not in any way the fruit of long deliberations, but rather a flowering of an unexpected second spring " (Pope John, *L'Osservatore Romano*, July 10, 1959).

Perhaps the greatest value of these Preparatory Reports of the preconciliar Commissions, composed almost entirely of members of the Roman Curia, lies in the contrast between their perspectives and the orientations, not only of Pope John but also and equally of the great majority of the fathers of the Council. This contrast seems to be based on two different conceptions of the relationship of the teaching mission of the church to her pastoral mission.

One conception of this relationship — in fact, the prevailing concept manifested in these Preparatory Reports — emphasizes the immutability and transhistorical validity of truth. Consequently, it sees the first duty of the teaching church to be the presentation of unchangeable truths in clear, timeless, and universally valid formulations, together with the condemnation of all deviations. The task of translating these unchangeable and abstract teachings into contemporary idiom, however, is not the function of the Magisterium. For if the teaching church herself were to present her doctrine in the language and thought patterns of the day, there is danger that she would expose these teachings to the give-and-take of historical change.

A second conception, expressed by Pope John himself at the beginning of the Council, emphasizes that the teaching mission of the church is itself essentially pastoral. This idea follows from the pastoral nature of revelation, directed as it is to men and to their salvation, expressed in human language and thought, yet without the loss of its unique and transcendental character. And just as God's revelation is at the service of his salvific will, so the teaching office of the church is subordinate to her pastoral goal of salvation. Pope John's inaugural address invited the Council to formulate the teachings of the church in a positive attempt to answer the questions of our modern world, and not to condemn those who question her statement of doctrine.

The perspectives of Pope John have prevailed. As a result, perhaps the most salient characteristic of the Council, expressed unmistakably by the vast majority of the fathers of the

Council, and preeminently by the two presiding popes, John XXIII and Paul VI, is its marked orientation toward a fruitful dialogue with the modern world in all its aspirations, personal, social, cultural, technical, and religious. This clear orientation is the key for understanding the three sessions of the Council, and undoubtedly it will be dominant in the fourth and final session.

This orientation disclosed itself most significantly by the fact that moments after his election as pope, Cardinal Montini, to show his identity with the spirit of Pope John, unhesitatingly and firmly chose the name of Paul to honor the apostle of the Gentiles, who was the first to break through the barriers and confining traditions of Israel's religion and to offer the good news of universal salvation in Christ to all men. There are many other unmistakable manifestations of this basic orientation: the presence of distinguished Protestant and Orthodox leaders at all sessions of the Council; the truly pioneering work of the Secretariat for Promoting Christian Unity under the wise and gentle leadership of Augustin Cardinal Bea; the establishment of a secretariat for non-Christians; the two voyages of Pope Paul to the Holy Land and to India; his frequent personal audiences with Christians of other confessions, with non-Christians, with world leaders in the fields of science, culture, technology, politics, and art.

In his major discourses, Pope Paul returns constantly to this dynamic orientation of the Council: " With these and other initiatives taken by us, we hope to have given clear witness to the universal dimensions of the church, which, in these times and in the climate of the Council, has not only strengthened her own interior bonds of love and brotherly cooperation but has equally sought to initiate and foster a plan of continuing dialogue and encounter with all men of goodwill " (L'Osservatore Romano, June 23, 1964).

The fathers of the Council and the two great Pontiffs who have inspired and guided its course thus far are saddened by their keen awareness that the modern world is estranged from

God and from the church. We live in what is, in many respects, a pagan world, and this pagan atmosphere, where it
exists in Western cultures, is not ignorance, but a rejection of
Christianity. This is the tragedy of modern man in contrast to
the pagan of St. Paul's age. The pagans of the Roman Empire
found in Christianity a novel hope and expectation of salvation. The modern pagan of the West thinks that he has known
Christianity and that he is fully justified in his disillusionment;
he looks upon it as a dragging weight of chains impeding his
personal fulfillment and has sought freedom by rejecting it
totally.

In reality, however, the modern pagan has not really known
or experienced authentic Christianity, and in his rejection he
has cast away only caricatures and grotesque presentations that
mask and disguise the true face of Christianity. The crisis culmination in this tragic rejection was sown centuries ago with
the birth of secularism at the end of the Middle Ages; it was
nurtured by the rediscovery of classical pagan humanism, the
Renaissance, the *Aufklärung,* and by the sweeping cultural
changes of the eighteenth and nineteenth centuries. In this
climate of his cultural heritage, modern man has grown to
adulthood outside the church, even though not always opposed
to her; hence his feelings of estrangement from Christianity.
During these long years, the church herself, hemmed in on all
sides and encircled by violent assaults bent on her destruction,
sought to preserve her life by enclosing herself in an em-
battled fortress of seclusion and withdrawal. Thus, between
the church and the world there was created a vast and deep
chasm.

On the other hand, however, there is in the modern world a
hidden nostalgia for Christianity. There exists a confused desire for the church, a profound thirst for those words of salvation which she alone can utter, and a consuming hunger for
those gestures of hope which she alone is empowered to perform. There is a growing sentiment in our crucial times that
perhaps Christianity still has something to address to modern

man, and that she has in her treasury solutions that can relieve the tensions of our great, though tragic, era.

Moreover, the church herself can no longer accept the position of existing in a besieged fortress: she is stirred to her
depths by the compelling need of pulverizing the walls and
barriers that have restricted her work of salvation; the Spirit
of God has inspired her with the imperative mission of bringing to men of our time, straitened by cataclysmic fears and by
the vertiginous pace of unprecedented change, her God-given
message of joy and peace in Christ, who has conquered the
world.

The short reign of Pope John XXIII responded remarkably
to the secret hopes of modern man and to the commanding
duty of the church to make her presence felt in the world. His
undying glory is, and will remain, that under the guidance of
the Spirit of God he tore down the wall of misunderstanding
and suspicion which divided the modern world from the
church, he dissolved the " besieged fortress " mentality by giving to the church a renewed breath of the Spirit through his
own ecumenical, universal, and authentically Catholic out-
look on all persons and things, and finally he opened up the
inexhaustible reaches of grace given to the church by Christ
and offered them to the world in such a spirit of humility and
charity that no man confronting the church now, whatever
his religion or lack of it, his race or his political and cultural
ideas, can any longer feel himself totally alienated and estranged from the dynamisms of authentic Christianity.

The Second Vatican Council, under the leadership of Paul
VI, has entered fully into the creative initiatives of John
XXIII and is striving vigorously to implement them, as the
following statement witnesses: " We look upon the world with
an unbounded sympathy. If the world feels estranged from
Christianity, Christianity does not feel itself alienated from
the world. Let the world know that it is esteemed and loved
by the Vicar of Christ, with a profound and inexhaustible love
— that love which is implanted in the very heart of the church

by our living faith. The Church has no other mission or goal than to be the servant and channel of God's immeasurable and ineffable love toward all men; the mission of the Church is to offer the friendship of God to man; it is a mission of understanding, of encouragement, of progress, of uplifting, and of salvation. We know that modern man prides himself on the creative genius of his scientific achievements whereby he has wrought hitherto unheard of and stupendous marvels. But these achievements have not made him a better human being; they have not made him one bit happier; they have not resolved human problems in their depth, in their vast extent, nor in their complexity. We know that modern man suffers from soul-searing doubts, from fogged-in obscurities, from excruciating anxieties. We offer him the word of salvation which alone can solve these frightening problems." (Pope Paul VI, Homily in Bethlehem, January 6, 1964.)

The strengthening word that Vatican II brings to a suffering world is the word of salvation, or, more truly, it is the Word who is the Savior himself: " Christ is the foundation of this Council. Christ is its way and guide. Christ is its hope and its goal. Our scrutiny of the world fills us with sadness. Atheism has invaded the hearts of many, and has established its inevitable disorientation of the moral, intellectual, and social orders. While the light of science has penetrated in our day more deeply into the hidden secrets of nature, at the same time there has developed an enshrouding darkness, obscuring the knowledge of God, and thereby rendering void any true knowledge of man in the depths of his dignity as a creature made unto the image and likeness of God. While scientific progress brings to perfection ever-more remarkable instruments for mastering nature, and places them at man's disposal, the heart of modern man, who has refused to be enlightened by God, has taken the downward path toward the void of sadness and despair." (Paul VI, Inaugural Address to the Second Session of Vatican II; L'Osservatore Romano, September 30, 1963.)

Nevertheless, the church sees in modern man not only the evils and sufferings caused by his estrangement from God but also the grandeur and nobility of his deepest aspirations toward peace and harmony. The church seeks to relieve his deep-seated anxieties and to fulfill his insatiable hunger for justice, for security, and for mutual harmony and cooperation among all peoples of the earth. Above all, the church is listening to the desperate plea for help which modern man, gropingly and without full awareness, directs to Jesus his Savior, because, notwithstanding his estrangement from God, modern man senses, at least implicitly and confusedly, that only the Second Adam, who is God enfleshed, can save him and bring it about that man's marvelous conquests of nature do not lead him to his own total obliteration. "We look out upon our troubled time, in all its complex and contrasting fluctuations, with deep compassion and with an ardent desire to offer to men of our time the good news of God's friendship and of that salvation which is Christ's testament and heritage to all mankind, entirely available to them if they will only receive it in living faith. Let all men know that the church regards them with profound compassion for their groping doubt and insecurity, with sincere admiration for their efforts to make this a better world for all men, and with an unbounded desire, not to subdue them, but to serve them, not to denigrate any truly human values or aspirations, but to value them as Christ does and to work for their fulfillment, not to condemn them, but to strengthen, console, and save them." (Paul VI, Inaugural Address; *loc. cit.*, September 30, 1963.)

The dialogue with the world undertaken by Vatican II is totally inspired with sympathy for and confidence in modern man; it is permeated with an all-embracing and indulgent understanding that springs forth, not from weakness, but from a profound and sincere humility, because it is inspired by the Spirit of Him who is meek and humble of heart. Vatican II does not present to the world a church driven on by unrealized dreams of triumphal domination over men's hearts, but a church desirous of becoming God's leaven in the one bread which is the mystical body of Christ, of witnessing herself as the herald and dispenser of God's saving truth, of being what God has willed her to be — the house of God on this earth, to which all men are invited to take up their abode, so that the children of God may be gathered from the ends of the earth in unity, to form one people, one body, one family of God. In a word, the mission of the church in Vatican II is prophetic, sanctifying, and saving.

The spirit of Vatican II aims at breaking down all unchristian barriers dividing mankind: the barriers of exaggerated nationalism, with its often not too subtle overtones of racial superiority so harmful in the past to the missionary efforts of the church; the barriers of false pride in family background or cultural status; the barriers of the dangerous (although all too often prevalent) assumption that narrowly inbred inherited prejudices, worldly standards of success, and other purely ephemeral values should constitute the basic foundation for our judgment or criticism of other individuals, other cultures, other nations, other races, and other religions.

What are the prospects for the continuation of a revitalized Christianity in the postconciliar years to come? The Spirit of God, who has given this new Pentecostal spirit, will not fail — but mankind must cooperate. We must remember constantly, both as individuals and collectively, that every Christian who is a member of Christ, and intimately united to him in love, continues and completes by all that he does in the Spirit of Jesus the work that Jesus began in the days of his flesh when he walked with men visibly on this earth. When such a Christian prays, his prayer is the continuation and fulfillment of the prayer of Jesus; when he suffers, the passion of Christ is reenacted in his body and spirit. In these troubled times, each Christian must recall constantly that he is unique, created to manifest to others a certain aspect of God's redeeming love which no other human person can show forth. There is one thing none of us may dare to list among his rights —

mediocrity; we are each irreplaceable, and it depends on each one of us whether the life of Jesus, given to us in Baptism, will flower into a rare and singular beauty, or become sickly and faded and finally wither and die. Our daily humdrum lives may seem as fleeting and unimportant as bubbles on a stream, but this is a dangerous delusion. For, to prolong the life of Christ in ourselves and in others, to radiate the magnetic charm of his beauty and love, as it is given us to do in his Spirit, is to inherit the earth and become fellow workers with God in the achievement of his divine will, so clearly manifested by Vatican II, that all men may be one in the mystical body.

Finally, all Christians must live, pray, and work in order that the postconciliar era may be guided by the Spirit of Him who said: " Learn of me, because I am meek, and humble of heart " (Matt. 11:29), and " The Son of man has not come to be ministered unto, but to minister to others, and to give his life, a redemption for many " (Mark 10:45). If this spirit prevails in the years after Vatican II, it will carry on the glorious renewal of life in Christ already begun, and will lead, slowly but surely, toward fulfilling Christ's will: " Father, that they all may be one in us, that the world may believe that thou hast sent me " (John 17:21).

In conclusion, may I express my sincere congratulations to the Reverend Aram Berard, S.J., for his scholarly and painstaking labor in making these important documents available to present and future historians of Vatican II, and my gratitude to him for allowing me to write this foreword.

Rev. Philip J. Donnelly, S.J.

Weston College
March 10, 1965

ACKNOWLEDGMENTS

I wish to express my sincere gratitude to all who helped me with this book: first, to Archbishop Martin O'Connor, president of the Vatican Council Press Service, for his courtesy in this matter, and to the editors of *La Documentation Catholique,* for permission to use their text; secondly, to all who helped me with the text itself, starting with the young men of the Boston College High School Sodality, who worked with me on these reports during 1962 and 1963, especially to Mr. Joseph Forina for his dedicated service; then to my Jesuit brothers at Weston College, especially to Mr. James Boland, S.J., for his help with the first draft, to Fr. John Walsh, S.J., and Fr. Francis Lawlor, S.J., for their advice on the project, to Fr. Philip Donnelly, S.J., for his fine foreword, and above all to Fr. Robert Farrell, S.J., for his generous help with the final copy.

The reports in this book were issued by the Vatican Council Press Service and published in *L'Osservatore Romano.* Here they are translated from the French version in *La Documentation Catholique* as follows:

First Session — T. LIX, No. 1, 372, March 18, 1962, col. 373 (note 1)

Second Session — T. LVIII, No. 1, 366, December 17, 1961, cols. 1565–1578

Third Session — T. LIX, No. 1, 370, February 18, 1962, cols. 235–250

Fourth Session — T. LIX, No. 1, 372, March 18, 1962, cols. 373–392

Fifth Session — T. LIX, No. 1, 375, May 6, 1962, cols. 571–592

Sixth Session — T. LIX, No. 1, 377, June 3, 1962, cols. 719–738

Seventh Session — T. LIX, No. 1, 380, July 15, 1962, cols. 905–927

Appendix I — List of Commissions and Secretariats — T. LVII, No. 1, 330, June 19, 1960, col. 710

Appendix II — Lists of Acts and Documents of the Antepreparatory Commission — T. LVIII, No. 1, 352, May 21, 1961, cols. 662–664

ARAM BERARD, S.J.

INTRODUCTION

By Aram Berard, S.J.

In order to place the Preparatory Reports in proper perspective, I should like to offer a brief account of the development of the Second Vatican Council and a note to the reader.

PREPARATION

On January 25, 1959, a few short weeks after his elevation to the See of Peter, Pope John XXIII announced his intention of convoking a council of the church universal.

An ecumenical council, as Pope John outlined it in his address on Pentecost Sunday, June 5, 1960, takes place in four stages. In the first stage, an antepreparatory commission initiates the conciliar process and establishes its guidelines. In the second stage, preparatory commissions draw up the schemata (drafts) and agenda for the council. (This phase is the subject of the Preparatory Reports.) The third stage is the actual celebration of the council carried out by the council fathers in conjunction with conciliar commissions. The last stage is the promulgation of the acts of the council and will require postconciliar commissions to carry out the decrees of the council.

Antepreparatory Commission

On May 17, 1959, four months after the announcement of the Second Vatican Council, Pope John appointed his secretary of state, Cardinal Tardini, to head the Antepreparatory Commission. Cardinal Tardini initiated this work the following month, on June 18, by inviting all the bishops, nuncios, vicars apostolic, prefects apostolic, and superiors general of religious orders and congregations to submit with complete liberty their suggestions and recommendations for the future Council.

By May 30, 1960, two thousand prelates had answered Cardinal Tardini's invitation. Their responses were added to the reports of the Roman Curia and of the Catholic universities throughout the world. The compilation of all this data comprised the preconciliar acts (*Acta*) and concluded the antepreparatory phase of the Second Vatican Council.

Preparatory Commissions

On Pentecost Sunday, June 5, 1960, Pope John issued a constitution establishing ten preparatory commissions and two secretariats. (See Appendix I.) Their task was to study the preconciliar *Acta* and to prepare schemata for the Holy Father and ultimately for the Council. The preparatory phase was officially opened on November 13, 1960, with the celebration of the Liturgy of St. John Chrysostom in the Byzantine-Slavonic rite. The following day, Pope John held a solemn audience for the cardinals, bishops, prefects, priests, and religious of the preparatory commissions and secretariats. On March 29, 1961, four volumes of the *Acta* and documents of the Antepreparatory Commission were published for use by these commissions. (See Appendix II.)

The meetings reported in the Preparatory Reports began on June 12, 1961, and ended on June 20, 1962. The Vatican Council Press Service issued these Reports in *L'Osservatore Romano* during the seven weeks of sessions held that year by the Central Preparatory Commission. (See Appendix III.) The final day of these reports brought the three years of preparation to a climax. During that period, seventy-three schemata were prepared and reviewed by the preparatory commissions. This was more than all the schemata of the previous twenty Ecumenical Councils put together. The Second Vatican Council, as Augustin Cardinal Bea recently stated (*The Catholic Messenger,* January 28, 1965), was the most extensive and best prepared Ecumenical Council in the history of the church.

CELEBRATION

First Session

As the Second Ecumenical Council of the Vatican opened on October 13, 1962, a storm cloud was forming over Cuba. The following week, on October 26, the Cuban Government authorized the USSR to build a Soviet port on the island. The threat loomed that war might end this Council just as the First Vatican Council had been ended by the Franco-Prussian War in 1870. Pope John sent an appeal for peace, which, according to recent observations (*Saturday Review,* February 13, 1965), had " a considerable effect on Chairman Khrushchev and the Russian people during the week of the Cuban crisis." Back in Rome, tensions penetrated deeply into the life of the church and positions were emerging that were to polarize the debates to come.

The immediate task facing the General Congregation (the general assembly of all the Council fathers in St. Peter's Basilica) was the crucial one of electing conciliar commission members, either from the Preparatory Commission staff or new members from the church at large.

The liturgy was the first subject to be considered. The schema on the sources of revelation was next on the agenda. After a week of lively debate on the sources of revelation, a vote was taken on November 21, to decide whether or not to eject the schema as a basis of discussion. The total rejection of the schema was voted for by 1,368 fathers and the continuation of the debate by 822. Father Yves Congar, O.P., called this event (*La Documentation Catholique,* November 1, 1964) the definitive end of the Counter-Reformation, because by a majority vote, the Council fathers decided to reject, on that day, a document on the sources of revelation which was too little ecumenical and still too much inspired by an anti-Protestant Catholicism. To reject the schema, however, a majority of 1,460 was required; and since the negative vote was 92 short of this number, the debate was due to continue. At this point Pope John ended the debate and set up a special mixed Commission composed of members of the Theological Commission and the Secretariat for Promoting Christian Unity. They were to rewrite the schema under the joint headship of Cardinal Ottaviani and Cardinal Bea. This marked the beginning of the reorganization and reintegration of the Preparatory Commissions' schemata.

The schema on communications was then briefly considered. This relaxed the tensions somewhat before the Council fathers directed their attention to the difficult questions of the church and church unity. When the question of ecumenism was proposed under different viewpoints (doctrinal and pastoral) by various Commissions (Theology, Oriental Churches, and Church Unity), it became necessary to have mixed commissions reorganize the matter.

A few days later, on December 5, the Council fathers received a leaflet listing twenty subjects taken from the seventy-three schemata of the Preparatory Commissions. These twenty subjects formed the new basis for the conciliar debates. The next day, Pope John issued directives for the revision of the schemata by each conciliar Commission. By the last day of the first session, December 7, the Council had become an instrument ready to begin the process of balloting on conciliar matter. The voting began on the Introduction and Chapter I of the liturgy schema.

The Coordinating Commission, nominated by the Pope on December 17, 1962, to take charge of the revision of the schemata, held two weeks of sessions (January 21–28 and March 25–29, 1963) during the interim before the second session of the Council. These meetings were held under the guiding hand of Pope John. On Pentecost Monday, June 3, 1963, after a few months' illness, Pope John XXIII died.

Slightly over two weeks later, on June 21, on the second day of conclave, John-Baptist Cardinal Montini was elected pope and took the name of Paul VI. The very next day, in his address to the world, Pope Paul announced that he would make the Second Vatican Council the main work of his pontificate.

Second Session

The second session of the Council opened on September 20, 1963. Over half of the agenda of this session was devoted to the schema considered the most important, *De ecclesia* (On the church). This schema was meant to be the ground in which all other constitutions and decrees would be rooted. The collegiality of bishops was the main issue of debate and was considered by some theologians of the Council to be the keystone of the modern church. The climax of this debate came on October 30, when the " historic " vote was taken on the " five questions." In the third of these questions, the Council fathers saw themselves as an episcopal college, in unity with its head the Roman Pontiff and never without him, to have full and supreme power over the universal church. The ensuing considerations on the schema on bishops and diocesan government was seen as flowing from the collegiality question of the *De ecclesia* schema.

The debates that followed on the liturgy schema centered on the issues of the vernacular and the concelebration of Mass. This constitution was accepted by the Council fathers on November 22, by a vote of 2,158 to 19 and promulgated by Pope Paul on December 4, 1963. On the same day, the pope promulgated the schema on communications. This decree was accepted by the fathers by a vote of 1,960 to 164. The final two weeks of the second session were devoted to the question of ecumenism.

During the interim before the third session, Pope Paul opened a new era in ecumenism on January 5, 1964, by his pilgrimage to the Holy Land and through his dialogue with His Holiness Athenagoras I, Patriarch of Constantinople. Thereafter, all the schemata yet to be debated were rewritten in accord with the suggestions of the fathers of the Council.

Third Session

The third session opened on September 15, 1964. During this session the Council fathers approved the *De ecclesia* constitution by a vote of 2,151 to 5 and Pope Paul promulgated it on November 22, 1964. On the previous day the pope had promulgated the decrees on the Oriental Churches and on ecumenism. All the various other schemata, dealing with the apostolate of bishops, priests, and laymen, with religious liberty, with the Jews and non-Christians, with religious orders, with revelation, and with the modern world, were presented and debated during this session.

A week before the end of the third session, on November 13, Pope Paul, moved by the presentation of the question of world poverty and the church's mission to the world, gave his tiara to the poor as a token of his concern for them. During the final hours of this session, the atmosphere became supercharged when a group of Council fathers pressed for an immediate vote on the issue of religious liberty. Pope Paul then decided to give this schema top priority at the fourth session.

During the interim before the fourth session, Pope Paul extended his ecumenical pilgrimage to the heart of India from December 2 to 5, 1964, on the occasion of the 38th International Eucharistic Congress then being held in Bombay. All the schemata yet to be approved were to be reworked in accord with the wishes of the Council fathers before the fourth and last session, opening on September 14, 1965. The fourth session brings the third phase of the Second Vatican Council to a close.

I hope this short account of the Council's development will provide a helpful context for the reader of the Preparatory Reports. Allow me to add one final note to the reader which may help him better appreciate the content of this book.

NOTE TO THE READER

The student of the Second Vatican Council could profitably keep in mind that the Preparatory Reports are *not* the reports of the Council itself, but of its Preparatory Commissions. This book represents the climax of the Council's preparatory phase. Its value can best be seen from a developmental point of view as containing the causes of, or in some cases the occasions for, what we now know to be the spirit of Vatican II.

Pope John commissioned the Roman Curia, as the central government of the church and the supreme administrative organ of the Holy See, to organize and prepare for this awesome undertaking. The pope's purpose in convoking the Council was to update (*aggiornamento*) the whole church. Both Pope John on April 12, 1962, and Pope Paul on September 21, 1963, issued documents indicating their deep concern for the updating of the Roman Curia itself. The Preparatory Reports represent a viewpoint that antedates these two documents.

Meetings of the Central Commission

FIRST SESSION

June 12, 1961, Pentecost Sunday

This first meeting took place in the Hall of the Congregations, on the third floor of the Apostolic Palace. Those attending were: 31 cardinals, 2 patriarchs, 72 archbishops and bishops, 23 Commission advisers, and 4 superiors of religious orders. This marked the beginning of a new phase in the preparation of the Council. This phase is most important because its main purpose is to examine the outlines prepared by each of the Commissions.

The Holy Father prayed to the Holy Spirit for help in the work of the Central Commission. The presidents of the Commissions were then asked to submit an account of their work. At this first meeting, the questions relevant to the celebration of the Council were examined. Pope John gave the opening address, in which he called on the presidents of the different Commissions to present their schemata to the Central Commission, and bring the presidents up to date on the work done. Monsignor Felici, secretary-general of the Central Commission, reported on the activities of this Commission. This first meeting was closed with a final address by Pope John and a prayer invoking the help of all the saints. (The function of the Central Commission is to study the questions related to the convocation of the Council. All the following meetings will be devoted to the examination of the outlines and schemata developed by each Commission.)

June 20, 1961 (Closing meeting of First Session)

The main objectives of the Council were discussed and brought to light. These are:

1. That all orders of the clergy might know a renewal (*aggiornamento*) of sanctity.
2. That the people should be instructed in the truth of faith and Christian morals.
3. That youth should be instructed and properly informed.
4. That the apostolic works of the social apostolate should be encouraged.
5. That all Christians should have a missionary spirit.
6. That all should have a fraternal and loving attitude toward all.

Monsignor Felici held a press conference for journalists of sixty nations concerning the first meeting of the Central Commission. He pointed out some questions demanding immediate attention. The order and procedure to be followed at the Council was also given, and runs as follows:

1. To convoke the various persons to the Council.
2. To bring together all the theologians and canonists who can benefit the Council.
3. To form constitutions for the conciliar Commission.
4. To order the proposed sessions and intermissions.
5. The majority vote required.
6. The language to be used during the Council (Latin, but others if necessary).
7. To record all Council discussions (i.e., by using mechanical devices and professional stenographers).

SECOND SESSION

THE PROFESSION OF FAITH

The opening report was read by Alfredo Cardinal Ottaviani, president of the Theological Commission. It concerned the new formulation of the profession of faith, which all fathers must pronounce by virtue of Canon Law before the sessions and conciliar discussions begin. A discussion by all assembled followed the reading of the report.

As in all the Councils, the agenda of the first meeting after the solemn opening ceremony is given to the profession of faith. If the new formula, foreseeing, among other things, the fusion of the profession of faith with the oath against modernism, is accepted, it will probably be adopted for the opening of the Council. We can, furthermore, suppose that it will be used in the future whenever its recitation is obligatory.

There is no question, obviously, of changing dogmas or adding new ones. The only question is one of new verbal expression to complete the formulation of all dogmatic truths that belong to the patrimony of faith.

The profession of faith dates back to the early centuries of Christianity. It was required of those about to receive Baptism. Then it soon became obligatory for candidates to sacred orders. The formula still in use, prescribed by Pius IV and modified by Pius IX in 1877, was the subject of today's discussion by the members of the Central Commission. (It was Pius IX who introduced the dogma of the immaculate conception and the definitions of the First Vatican Council.)

Later, in 1910, St. Pius X ordered that the profession of faith be not only read but also signed and followed by the oath against modernism. The persons who are held to make the profession of faith are listed in canon 1406.

November 10, 1961

THE CONSTITUTION
ON THE SOURCES OF REVELATION

The work of this third day centered upon the constitution on the sources of revelation. Alfredo Cardinal Ottaviani, president of the Theological Commission, gave the report. Because the secretaries of the interested Commissions were allowed to participate, Father Sébastien Tromp, S.J., professor at the Gregorian University, and secretary of the Theological Commission, was present this morning.

In the terminology of the Council, the word " constitution " is used for texts of doctrine. The word " decree " is used in disciplinary matters.

Before voting approval or rejection of the schema presented, the members and the counselors examined it and discussed it in detail. In order to avoid all equivocity, it may be helpful to repeat that when we speak of the approbation of a schema on the part of the Central Commission, it refers only to its acceptance for presentation to the Holy Father. It will thereafter be presented to the Council fathers. One must bear in mind that this is the Preparatory Commission of the Council, not the Council itself.

The schema on the sources of revelation, presented by Cardinal Ottaviani, is of primary importance because it examines the sources themselves from which our faith is nourished. In every age, and especially in recent years, numerous questions have arisen concerning this delicate subject. The Central Commission wanted to answer these carefully selected questions in their investigation of this schema.

It is obvious that God, at certain times in human history, spoke to man, and man was able to record this divine voice. This communication of the truth made directly by God to man is called " revelation."

There exist for us two sources from which men draw revealed truths: Holy Scripture, called the Bible, which contains the Old and New Testaments; and Tradition.

Holy Scripture contains all the truths that God dictated to man in order that man might transmit the written text to future generations. By enlightening the intellect and guiding the will of man, God made use of him as an instrument to make known by the hagiographer's words the divine and eternal truths that could not have been known by the light of unaided reason.

Tradition, on the other hand, contains the truths that were also revealed by God, but that were handed down from the beginning, generation to generation, by the spoken, not the written, word. These truths are contained today in the documents of the ecclesiastical magisterium and in the writings of the fathers and doctors of the church.

There are, then, two sources of revelation, but there is only one mysterious source from which they come. If we may so express ourselves, that origin is God. There is only one magisterium commissioned by virtue of a divine mandate to preserve and authentically interpret the truths contained in these sources. One may say, in fact, that Holy Scripture itself, while reporting the divine words, expresses them in human language. This language, by reason of all the imperfections and limitations of human means, often requires precise interpretations and authorized explanations in order to be understood. These cannot come simply from men who are equally imperfect and limited, but only from those who, by virtue of a faithful promise, are continually assisted by the Holy Spirit.

THE INVITATION
TO THE SEPARATED BROTHERS

The news concerning the first meeting of this autumn session of the Central Preconciliar Commission has brought about great interest. The attention of the press has particularly focused on the opportunity of inviting the separated brothers to assist at the celebration of the Council.

Members of the Central Commission have freely given their opinions on this question. After mature deliberation, they voted on two reports at the close of the discussion. These reports were presented by Cardinal Bea and Amleto Cardinal Cicognani, in their respective capacity as president of the Secretariat for Christian Unity and of the Commission for the Oriental Churches.

Needless to say, this is only a consultative vote, for it belongs exclusively to the Holy Father to make a definitive judgment on this important question. All that could be said one way or another would be premature, and consequently all speculation on the ways of inviting non-Catholics would be still more premature.

November 11, 1961

THE REPARTITION OF THE CLERGY
AMONG THE DIFFERENT DIOCESES

With this Saturday morning meeting, the first week's work of the Central Commission came to an end. As president of the Commission on the Discipline of the Clergy and the Christian People, Pietro Cardinal Ciriaci read a report on one of the most vital and urgent problems of the Catholic world: a better distribution of the clergy. This is in answer to the ever-growing needs of different areas in the matter of religious instruction and assistance.

This theme, which has often been studied in the past few years at national and international congresses, especially in Europe and Latin America, particularly interested the members and counselors of the Central Commission. A great number of these men daily experience a sad pastoral life. They are deprived of the essential means for accomplishing their mission from Jesus Christ of evangelizing all men. They see the dangers to which a great number of faithful are exposed in countries of old Catholic tradition as well as in countries newly born into the light of faith. Because of the lack of available priests, it is difficult even for those of goodwill to acquire a knowledge of fundamental truths and to frequent the sacraments. The teachings of the encyclicals *Fidei donum* of Pius XII and *Sacerdotii nostri primordia* and *Ad Petri cathedram* of John XXIII have profound echoes in the hearts of the successors of the apostles. They experience an urgent need, emphasized by St. Peter in his first epistle, to communicate grace to others.

Cardinal Ciriaci's report was listened to with great interest, and it provided grounds for constructive discussion. Rev. Cristoforo Berutti, O.P., professor at the Angelicum and secretary of the Commission on the Discipline of the Clergy and the Christian People, was also present.

INCARDINATION AND EXCARDINATION

It is natural that, in the examination of a schema to be presented to the Holy Father, the members and counselors would consider the prescriptions of Canon Law regulating the incardination and excardination of priests in and out of their respective dioceses.

Canon Law demands that there be no priests without a fixed abode. All priests must be subject to a determined superior and be at the service of a diocese. The act by which a candidate to the ecclesiastical state is normally incorporated into the diocesan clergy, thereby conferring a new kind of religious citizenship on him, is called " incardination." The passage from one diocese to another, subject to the rule of Canon Law, is called " excardination." There can be no excardination from one diocese without an immediate incardination into another.

Since apostolic times there has been an obligation not to ordain a priest except for service in a specific church. Since Nicaea, in 325, many Councils have confirmed these directives. The Council of Chalcedon, in 451, went as far as to declare invalid the ordination of errant or acephalic priests. Eleven hundred years later, the Council of Trent, by reason of some abuses on this point, recalled the prescriptions and sanctions of the Council of Chalcedon.

Rules as old and wise as these could certainly not be abolished. However, there is nothing to hinder the study of a schema to be presented to the Holy Father concerning a more equitable distribution of the clergy among the different Catholic countries. This study would be done with the needs of the missionary world in mind.

A recent statistic taken from this year's *L'Annuario Pontificio* shows that we range from a maximum of one priest for five hundred Catholic inhabitants to a minimum of one priest for more than eleven thousand inhabitants.

VOCATIONS

Closely related to this problem is the one of ecclesiastical vocations, which has not been treated today by the Central Commission. But to clarify this complex question, these are a few figures recently cited at a congress for ecclesiastic vocations by Giuseppe Cardinal Pizzardo, the prefect of the Sacred Congregation of Seminaries and Universities. In eleven hundred dioceses, having relations with the Sacred Congregation of Seminaries, we count 228,653 priests for 418,000,000 Catholics and a global population of 692,000,000 people. For a homogeneous distribution of one priest to every thousand Catholics, 190,000 more priests are needed. For a ratio of one priest to every thousand persons, no matter what their religion might be, 470,000 more priests are needed.

In view of this situation, the prayer of Christ asking God to send laborers into the harvest comes immediately to mind. It is by this prayer that all the faithful can collaborate in the success of the Central Commission's work, even though this work, understandably enough, must be done in secret.

November 13, 1961

PRIESTLY SANCTITY

The schema presented today concerned the intimate life of the priest and his specific duty of growing in sanctity. The report was, again, given by Pietro Cardinal Ciriaci, prefect of the Sacred Congregation of the Council, and president of the Commission on the Discipline of the Clergy and the Christian People.

The church is holy, according to the definition of the Council of Constantinople (381), and she remains so even if some of her members are far from being holy. Her holiness comes from her divine institution and from her mission to lead those who are docile to perfection. Sanctity does not come from the qualities of her sons. This means that all the faithful, and in particular the priests, must be conscious of their duty to be saints. This duty is inherent not only in their baptism but also in their ordination. The Roman Synod recalls this duty in many articles, as for example in these words of Pius XII: " By the sacrament of Orders, God has concluded a pact of eternal love with the priest and he asks sanctity in return." This, therefore, should be his most splendid characteristic.

It happens at times, in following the attractions of an extreme superficiality, that the organs of information stress marginal questions, e.g., those concerning the habit. These are stressed rather than the fundamental questions, e.g., the interior life of the priest, his practice of the ascetical virtues, and his fidelity to the promises of his priesthood. The priest's true reality and grandeur certainly does not reside in his habit, as sacred as this may be. But it is found in his daily constant search for a holier life, especially in the practice of obedience, chastity, and detachment from worldly goods. This is done in spite of the world's pressure in the midst of which he lives, and in spite of the moral dangers that surround him on all sides.

Pontifical documents on this question have increased in the last century. Since *Haerent animo* of Pius X to *Sacerdotii nostri primordia* of John XXIII along with his many allocutions, to *Ad Catholici sacerdotii* of Pius XI and *Menti nostrae* of Pius XII, one can say that the sovereign pontiffs have held this preoccupation closest to their heart. Their vigilance over the clergy is without interruption, lest their priests deviate from the straight and narrow path of a good life, by accepting erroneous doctrines, or by following the attractions of illicit novelties. Modernism had a tragic effect on the church, depriving her of many of her sons' beautiful energies. Unfortunately, illusory ideologies and dangers renew themselves with the passing generations. These always possess the power of attracting not only the laity but also the priest. This happens if both do not aspire to an ever-greater union with God and a more profound spirit of obedience to the hierarchy.

Obviously this is not a new problem. Even at the time of the Old Law, God demanded that his priests be better than the other members of his people because of the nature of their functions and their special relationship with the Lord. These imposed a sanctity on them which Holy Scripture constantly recalls, even in severe language at times. In instituting the priesthood of the new law, Jesus insisted in the gospel on the fundamental idea expressed in his prayer at the Last Supper:

"And for these I sanctify myself in order that they also may be sanctified in truth."

St. Peter wants the ministers of God to be like the matrix on which the faithful are formed. St. Paul summarizes all his teaching in this invitation: "Be ye imitators of me as I am of Christ." Patristic literature is rich in reproving the priest for all that might obscure his sanctity, and teaches the duty of tending to perfection. To limit ourselves only to the ancient fathers and doctors, let us mention: *De sacerdotio* of St. John Chrysostom, *De officiis* of St. Ambrose, *De ecclesiastica hierarchia* of St. Denys, the Pseudo-Areopagite, and the *Regulae pastoralis liber* of St. Gregory the Great. In his synthetic Latin, St. Thomas Aquinas goes as far as to say that the priest must be in his holiness: "*deiformissimus et Deo similimus*" (most like to God).

The whole liturgy of the sacrament of Orders is also filled with invitations to priestly holiness. This holiness is mentioned in canon 124 of the Code: "The priest must have a more holy interior and exterior life than the laity, and he must always offer them an example in the practice of virtues and good works."

What did the Central Commission do yesterday? It has certainly not decided radical reforms in discipline, but it has studied more deeply the means of a spiritual order destined to make the priest progress more courageously along the road to sanctity. This he must do while living in a world pagan in many ways, but a world that must be completely conquered for Christ.

As the Holy Father has often emphasized, one of the ends of the Council is "to nourish a supernatural sense in every member of the priesthood and the laity and to adapt the ecclesiastical discipline to the needs of our times for the greater sanctification of the clergy and the edification of the Christian people. We expect great things from the Council: a vigorous renewal in faith, doctrine, ecclesiastical discipline, religious and spiritual life. If all this is to be realized, we must obviously start with the clergy." This was why yesterday's meeting of the Central Commission was so important.

November 14, 1961

PARISHES

Continuing the study of themes already prepared by the Commission on the Discipline of the Clergy and the Christian People, presided over by Pietro Ciriaci, the members and counselors of the Central Commission examined a schema of decree on the provision, the union, and the division of parishes.

During this seventh day of the session, Cardinal Tisserant presided and Cardinal Ciriaci reported on the schema.

After mentioning the less important questions of the cassock and tonsure, the Commission attentively studied the more important problem of parish life in modern society. Society has undergone radical evolution and transformation because of urbanism, rapid transportation, tourist trade, and leisure-time activities.

This subject must be related to the one presented two days ago on priestly sanctity. The priest, in fact, does not consecrate himself to a contemplative life, but to an active one with all the demands of the pastoral ministry. The sanctity of the priest should, therefore, manifest itself in his teaching, his spiritual action, and his example. This is done in most cases by the exercise of his parochial ministry. Each priest, whatever his duty may be, is obliged to tend to sanctity. But we can say, in a certain sense, that the pastor of the parish has this obligation for two reasons: for his own salvation and for the edification of the people entrusted to him.

Concerning the Blessed Innocenzo da Berzo, who was a diocesan priest before becoming a Capuchin, the Holy Father last Sunday mentioned these truths relevant to our subject: " We like to offer him as an example, especially to priests, to religious, to seminarians, and to consecrated souls, because it is especially there that the secret of all effective apostolate is found. He was given primarily to prayer, penance, and sincere humility, that is to say, sanctity."

In recent times, many studies have been made regarding the constitutional aspects of the parish. In its essential lines the parish system dates back to the sixth century. The question is whether this structure is still functional today for instructing, sanctifying, and saving souls, or whether it has become outmoded for this task. By studying ways of more adequately meeting the needs of the parish, the Central Commission has implicitly approved the parish structure. The same approval is implied in the Commission's concern for grouping undersized parishes together as well as for dividing those which are too wealthy.

Canon Law, moreover, indicates the great importance of the parish, by devoting its longest rubrics to the notions of " parish " and " pastor." The Code says, among other things, that each diocese must be divided into parishes and that these smallest territorial units of the church must be entrusted to the priests who are the most learned as well as the most gifted in all the qualities necessary for the progress of souls.

Evidently, from these brief notes, the subject discussed yesterday by the Central Commission, before being presented to the Holy Father, is a fundamental one on which rests the very mission of the church. The church must contact every soul, and its organization must be the most complete for answering, in the best possible way, the needs of the time. By condemning the interference of the laity in claiming rights to nominate their pastors and by reaffirming the parochial discipline of the church's noble origins, the Council of Trent made the parish one of the firmest pivots of the Catholic reform. The Second Vatican Council, now setting down the principles of adaptation, will show how the time-honored parochial structure is still valid today.

November 16, 1961

THE DUTIES OF PASTORS

The Central Commission adjourned its meeting today in order to permit each member and counselor to prepare privately his observations on the schemata remaining for discussion.

During yesterday's session, after the questions on the provision, union, and division of parishes were completed, the Commission started to discuss a schema of decree on the manifold duties of pastors. The Code of Canon Law especially emphasizes: the duty of residence so that pastors may know their faithful better and so that they may always be at their disposal; the duty to say Mass *pro populo* on Sundays and prescribed feast days; the duty of administering the Sacraments; and the duty of providing religious instruction.

The Latin *parochus* (pastor) probably comes from the Greek verb meaning " to live together." The pastor, then, is the one who lives in the midst of his faithful. This word has been frequently used since the Council of Trent. Previous to it, the priests in charge of souls were not called pastors, but their titles varied according to the place. They were called archpriests, pastors, priors, rectors, plebians, etc. Certain of these titles still exist today with the same, or a slightly different, meaning. The pastor has been an institution in the church since the fourth century. The provincial council of Arles, in 314, asked that priests live in the country with their people.

In addition to the habitual duties of pastors, others are being added daily, causing the pastor to face the new circumstances in urban, industrial, and tourist centers.

All kinds of attractions offered by the world in an immoral and amoral atmosphere penetrate even into the most Christian of families. These require a highly spiritual, intellectual, and moral preparation on the part of the pastors to help them resist this insidious propaganda and offer to their faithful a truly visible presence of God in their midst. In urban centers where the most appealing expressions of life attract to evil, the pastors remain the only reminder of spiritual realities.

For certain persons excessive work can constitute an ever-present danger of abandoning themselves to a zeal that borders on frivolity and superficiality. For others, solitude could represent a tendency toward indolence and discouragement. The Roman Synod had already asked pastors to observe a proper hierarchy of value. They should make use of prayer and especially meditation, monthly recollections, retreats, and also enter into a common life with their nearest collaborators, inasmuch as this is possible, so that they might become true pastors of souls. And, furthermore, following the example of the Divine Pastor, they should consecrate all their self-sacrificing energies to the search for and defense of those souls redeemed by the blood of Christ confided to their care.

The schemata proposed for discussion to the Central Commission today by Cardinal Ciriaci, president of the Commission on the Discipline of the Clergy and the Christian People, are logically bound together and constitute an integral whole. In the first place, there is the pressing need for a better distribution of the clergy to answer the exigencies of too great a number deprived of spiritual assistance; there is the need for priests to be holy in order that they might perform useful parish functions, for the need of such priests grows deeper and greater every day. The labors of the parochial ministry will be fruitful to the extent that priests are truly priests, both on a natural and supernatural level.

THE PREPARATION OF THE COUNCIL CONCERNS ALL CATHOLICS

The Episcopal Italian Conference, which met recently in Rome under the presidency of Cardinal Siri, published a communiqué at the close of its sessions in which the Italian cardinals and bishops, conscious of their pastoral duties, invited

" the whole world to a serious and generous reform of private and public morals, which will equally be a worthy preparation for the Ecumenical Council. Because this Council will be held in Rome, it will be a matter of great honor for the Italian Catholics, but above all, will point up their special responsibility to the world."

This is an aspect of the preparation of the Council which we easily tend to forget: the Council is an event that concerns the whole world, cleric and lay; it must then be prepared for by everyone's daily effort to improve, according to each one's proper responsibilities.

The Central Commission and individual Commissions undertake a great work in elaborating and drafting the schemata to be presented to the pope. But there is a work that requires still more attention and extends to all who wish to be united with the mind of the church by participating in these great events with a greater magnanimity of soul.

The Council will be, in fact, efficacious in the spiritual renewal continually desired by the Holy Father, to the extent that all Catholics make the pope's objective their own from now on. The Council could not act as a purely external force in presenting new constitutions and new decrees. It must become, however, a ferment that incites to a renewal of life, even before its actual celebration. The Holy Father is more explicit on this subject. " Our efforts and works," he says, " to make the Council a great event would be in vain if this collective effort of sanctification were not sufficiently unanimous and freely chosen."

THE ECCLESIASTICAL
OFFICES AND BENEFICES

The works of the Central Commission ended with the two last expositions of Cardinal Ciriaci. Yesterday the discussions dealt with the ecclesiastical offices, benefices, and the administration of church property. These matters are very juridical and of limited interest to the ordinary man.

By ecclesiastical office we mean all posts of a stable character for a spiritual good. There are offices of divine institution such as those of the Supreme Pontiff and residential bishops. The great majority of ecclesiastical offices are of human institution. Some, however, date back to the first centuries of the church, whereas others were created later in order to meet the needs of the times and of specific places.

The ecclesiastical benefice is defined by the Code of Canon Law as " a juridical entity constituted or erected with a perpetual title by the competent ecclesiastical authority, comprising a sacred office with the right to collect the endowed revenue of this office " (canon 1409). As with every precisely defined institution, this institution is characterized and distinguished in its essential elements. Its juridical personality is derived uniquely from the will of ecclesiastical authority, even though a layman may offer the endowment. This is an institution without time limit. Its essential elements are: the office, established for the maintenance of its title; the endowment, as the basis of its patrimony; and the revenues to provide for the support of the beneficiary, for the preservation and renewal of the benefice, for the help of the poor, and for the development of charitable works.

Again according to Canon Law, the benefice — and in part, the offices — can be: consistorial, if they are conferred by the Sacred Congregation of the Consistory, the others being nonconsistorial; secular, if they concern only diocesan priests; religious, if they are attributed to priests of religious orders; residential or nonresidential, insofar as their title is attached to a residence or not; movable or nonmovable, inasmuch as they are conferred to a revocable or perpetual title, with or without the care of souls.

Canon 1472 says that the priest " beneficiary, after taking legitimate possession of his benefice, profits from the temporal and spiritual rights annexed to it." And at the same time, he accepts all those duties which are attached to or flow from it and especially those for which the benefice was created.

The administration of the benefice property belongs to the beneficiary, who must see to it that the revenues are consumed or distributed without diminishing the patrimony.

We must not be astonished at the interest that the Central Commission as well as the Commissions on the Discipline of the Clergy and on the Sacraments, and the Code of Canon Law itself, have in these realities and problems of a purely material nature. There is a hierarchy of values that guides the preparatory work of the Council in this field as in others. The fundamental questions are first studied, i.e., those of a spiritual order, e.g., priestly holiness, then the less important but still necessary questions such as that of ecclesiastical benefices.

By his mission, the priest is a detached man. His life must be consecrated not to his own welfare but to that of others, to a spiritual ideal and not to the quest for material goods. He is, nevertheless, a man with material needs that cannot be ignored, both for his own support and for his pastoral ministry.

The necessity, therefore, arises for the priest to be free of the responsibility of earning his daily bread by works which would be unbecoming to his priestly dignity and which would take time away from his pastoral ministry for which he is consecrated. This principle was again confirmed on the occasion of the recent problems that have arisen concerning the new forms of the apostolate.

The benefice has always had the support, sustenance, and maintenance of the office as its specific end. If offices were at times created without benefices, there has never been a benefice created without its purpose being of a spiritual order, wanted by the church for the vitality and development of the priestly ministry. If at times in history, civil authorities have tried to subject the clerics to their own interests by attaching these benefices to nonreligious purposes, the church has vigorously reacted by claiming the independent and uniquely spiritual character of her mission. The "quarrel of universities" can be cited here as an example and a witness of the attitude that the church has maintained through the centuries in order to preserve the sacred character of ecclesiastical benefices.

THE HISTORICAL AND ARTISTIC ECCLESIASTICAL PATRIMONY

In the last part of the June 16 meeting, the Central Commission also examined a schema on the archives and the ecclesiastical libraries. Pietro Cardinal Ciriaci again reported on this last question.

THE ARCHIVES

The word " archives," slightly losing its Greek origin, means a collection of documents, usually gathered together for the purpose of historical documentation. Everyone knows of the existence of civil and ecclesiastical archives. Among the first, let us mention only the archives of the state, the notarial archives, etc. Among the latter, there are the pontifical archives; the diocesan archives, partly public and partly secret (the latter can be consulted by the bishop alone) ; the parochial archives, where the registers, the state of souls, the official communications, and certain important correspondence are preserved.

The church has always taken special care of archives. We can add that during these past few decades she has been particularly concerned in preserving them and defending them zealously. In Italy, for example, a first census of the ecclesiastical archives was made in 1942. Unfortunately, during World War II, 779 archives in Italy alone were destroyed; fifty-three of these were diocesan.

LIBRARIES

The Central Commission, along with the questions of the archives, also studied the related question of libraries. The

Greek origin of this word indicates a collection of books for consultation and study.

History recalls with admiration the ancient libraries of Alexandria, Pergamum, Athens, and Rome. During the period of the Roman Empire, libraries became as much a necessity of life as the stadium and the baths.

The first Christians took special care to keep the books of Sacred Scripture, the acts of the martyrs, the letters of popes and bishops, the liturgical rubrics, the list of churches and communities of sisters scattered throughout the world. We know, in fact, from St. Jerome the distrust of converts for books of philosophy and pagan literature because of what they contained contrary to Christian truth and morals.

It was Western monasticism, with its patriarch St. Benedict, that reestablished among Christians the interest in all books. Monasteries quickly became the guardians and defenders of the ancient parchments in which the sources of civilization were found.

Among the well-known ecclesiastical libraries, let us mention the Vatican and the Ambrosian libraries, the diocesan libraries, those of the monasteries, seminaries, religious orders, and universities. These are often valuable. They can be considered the source of much historical research and they often contain valuable parchments, early printed books, colored prints, manuscripts, and parchment tablets. This rapid survey allows us to understand why the Central Commission thought it worthwhile to bring the archives and libraries to the attention of the clergy.

SACRED ART

The last subject examined in yesterday's meeting was that of art, or rather, monuments and artistic works, which are ecclesiastical property or are kept in churches or religious houses.

The church has condemned the Iconoclast heresy and has used art for the instruction and education of the faithful. The

Council of Trent has clearly defined the sacred character of creative art that is destined for church use. By forbidding daring, unbecoming, or truculent paintings and sculpture, and by recommending a well-understood veneration of images, the church has given a new impetus to all art that elevates the soul and leads to prayer.

Without entering into the numerous polemics occasioned by modern art, let us refer to the words of Pius XII in *Mediator Dei:* " The modern works must not be entirely disregarded and rejected a priori, but while avoiding the excesses of realism and symbolism on the one hand, with a wise spirit of proportion, one must also keep the needs of the Christian community in mind rather than the personal judgment and tastes of the artist. It is, furthermore, extremely important to give freedom to modern art."

The works of the autumn session of the Central Commission came to a close on the study of this last schema.

CONCLUSION

The same issue of *L'Osservatore Romano,* November 19, 1961, completed its report of this session in the following manner. The pope was not able (as he greatly desired) to preside at each meeting because of his many important audiences and his other activities. He followed, however, the development of the works daily by becoming personally familiar with all that was said and proposed in each of the schemata. There were eight meetings during which ten schemata were submitted to the Central Commission for consideration. We must note that all the schemata had been previously sent to the members and counselors for advance study to allow them to draft their observations in writing. The schemata discussed by the Commission will again be elaborated by the competent subcommissions, keeping in mind the propositions and suggestions of the Central Commission.

THIRD SESSION

January 15, 1962

THE MORAL ORDER

We know that the morals and precepts of the Christian life must be based on the truths of revelation. This requires that faith be accompanied by practice in a perfect cohesion. Faith without works is dead, said St. Paul.* The principles of natural morality themselves are absorbed and perfected by Christian morality. This latter has the specific end of leading men to God by the precepts that regulate all the actions of man, from the innermost movements of soul to exterior acts, from private acts to those done in public, in the very exercise of one's profession or trade.

It is becoming more evident even among believers that there is a form of moral disorder in which the limits between good and evil become confused and even disappear. Such is also the case between what is just and unjust, between truth and error, and between what is licit and what is not. Pius XII declared in one of his discourses that the greatest sin of our time is not to believe in sin, i.e., no longer to believe in the existence of the moral order that qualifies and distinguishes the thoughts, affections, and human actions before God. From this disorder are born errors denying the existence of God, the

* Translator's Note: James 2:17 seems to be intended here.

author and guardian of the moral order. The attempt is then made, varying with men and time, to substitute the useful, the agreeable, the good of the race, the interests of a class, or the power of the state, as the criterion of morality. Thus, philosophical systems, literary fashions, and political doctrines have been created and propagated. These try to substitute for the Christian moral order the so-called morality of situation or individualistic morality, often condemned by Pius XII and finally condemned by a decree of the Holy Office in February of 1956. These also try to substitute the morality of independence (i.e., divorced from the Christian morality) for the idea of God, sanction, and obligation.

Naturally the deleterious consequences of these theories are always reflected in the conscience of people, whether they are aware of it or not. So it is that some speak with an extreme liberality of the autonomy of conscience or of the direct conversations between conscience and God without the intermediary of laws and religion, as if these were an obstacle. One so frequently hears discussions today on the so-called conflicts in reality between art and morality, or between freedom of expression and conscience. These conflicts have been artificially created and indicate the errors which have permeated many minds.

In the final analysis, this matter concerns errors which degrade human dignity under the false pretext of freeing man from all bonds that would restrict his nature in some way. The moral order has the task, not only of leading man to his true end, but of defending him against all doctrines and practices that would enslave him to the minds, modes, and passions that are contrary to the dignity of his intellect.

In particular, the moral order defends the immutable principles of Christian modesty and chastity. We know the energies spent at the present time by the world of fashion, movies, and the press in order to shake the foundations of Christian morality in this regard, as if the Sixth Commandment should be considered outmoded and free rein should be given to all passions, even those against nature. The Council will have something to say concerning this subject. It will clarify and eventually condemn all the attempts to revive paganism and all the trends that in the abuse of psychoanalysis tend to justify even those things which are directly contrary to the moral order.

As we can well imagine, this is a vast field which the Central Commission explored today. It is especially a domain in which the most diverse errors multiply, favored by the conditions of the modern world: by its technical progress, its modes of life, and its growing means of propaganda and publicity. Far from losing itself in speculation and losing contact with daily life, the Commission turns toward modern man, toward the spiritual dangers that surround him, and it penetrates resolutely to the heart of the problem, in order to indicate the practical and sure ways that lead to salvation.

January 16, 1962

THE SACRAMENT OF CONFIRMATION

After hearing the general report presented by Cardinal Aloisi Masella, president of the Commission on the Discipline of the Sacraments, the Central Commission studied two schemata: one on the sacrament of Confirmation, and the other on the sacrament of Penance.

Confirmation is the second sacrament of the Christian life, the complement of Baptism and the preparation for Communion. The two Italian words by which it is designated indicate its meaning: *cresima* is the matter and the unction made by the bishop on the forehead of the faithful; and the second, *confermazione,* indicates the fruit of the sacrament, i.e., the confirmation of the virtue of faith received as a seed in Baptism. In antiquity, the word " consignation " was used more frequently. This term better explains the definitive admission of the confirmed among the Christian people.

In the Latin Church from the first centuries, and then in a more evident manner after the thirteenth century, Confirmation was separated from Baptism and conferred at a later time only by a bishop. It is only in the Spanish-speaking countries that Confirmation is still administered to infants. In the Greek Church the anointing with holy chrism has always been given immediately after Baptism by a simple priest.

During these past few years, congresses and ecclesiastical reviews have discussed the question of the most opportune age at which to administer Confirmation. There is a tendency, especially for pastoral motives, that would want to delay Confirmation until the twelfth or fifteenth year, thereby arbitrarily making it the sacrament of Christian adolescence. There is another tendency, better supported by theological, historical, and juridical motives, that insists on the maintenance of the seventh year as the best for the reception of Confirmation, while recommending that it be preceded by the reception of the Eucharist. The Twelfth Italian Liturgical Week, held at Assisi in July of 1961, states that where it is pastorally possible, the traditional order of the sacramental itinerary should be preserved, having Confirmation before first Communion. This makes the Eucharistic banquet appear as the culmination and the guarantee of faithful perseverance in the spiritual edifice, having its foundation in Baptism and sacramental complement in Confirmation. Since it is highly recommended, therefore, to have children approach the Eucharist at the age of reason, that age is also indicated as the most convenient for Confirmation.

Besides this interesting aspect from a theological and pastoral point of view, the Central Commission examined other problems pertaining to the sacrament of Confirmation: the preparation and responsibility of godparents, the opportunity of extending the power of administering Confirmation to non-episcopal ministers by making the September 14, 1946, decree of the Sacred Congregation of the Sacraments more easily applicable. This decree was approved by the Holy Father, who had already given the power to pastors and curates to administer Confirmation in case of necessity. Because of the scarcity of the clergy and the exigencies of modern life, it is necessary to facilitate, as much as possible, the frequent reception of the sacraments which were instituted for men, i.e., to help them attain their end and eternal salvation.

THE POWER TO HEAR CONFESSIONS

In this matter, likewise, the Central Commission was not concerned with the aspects of this sacrament's divine institution, since these are indisputable. Nor was it interested in questions of this sacrament's validity or efficacy in achieving the end wanted by the Savior for all times and for all people. It was, rather, concerned with the juridical aspects of the powers that priests have to hear confessions. The rapid means of communication now permitting long and frequent travels, as well as motives taken from daily pastoral life, suggest that everything which would make the practice of the sacrament of Penance difficult and troublesome should be restrained as much as possible. Evidently there is no question, as some might think, of minimizing this sacrament. This sacrament entails the spirit of faith and demands particular dispositions. The question here is to suppress those obstacles which make it difficult to have priests at the disposal of souls desirous of grace, especially while on trips and pilgrimages, or during congresses.

January 17, 1962

SACRED ORDERS — HELP FOR PRIESTS

As was done yesterday for the sacraments of Confirmation and Penance, so today the interest of the Central Commission was not centered on the substance or divine institution of the sacraments, which are really part of the acquired patrimony of faith and for which the definitions of the Council of Trent retain their complete vitality and present-day interest. The Commission studied, rather, the vital though secondary aspects of the sacrament of Orders, in order to adapt the activity of the clergy to the exigencies of modern life. This is to be done, however, without excluding the opportunity of renewing the institutions established since the first centuries of the church for the pastoral needs of our day. The results of this morning's discussion, which were surrounded with a proper reserve, are not definitive and have not yet been disclosed to us. We can, however, illustrate in a generic way the historical and theological context in which this question is to be viewed.

Our Lord instituted the power to renew the unbloody sacrifice of the Mass, the power to remit sins, and the mission to instruct, sanctify, and govern all peoples, by conferring these powers on the apostles, and through them, upon their successors.

The apostles had the fullness of these priestly powers, but they soon chose subordinates to whom they transmitted a part of their power. These latter were the priests.

Then by reason of the growing need for assistance in the apostolate, The Acts of the Apostles record that the twelve convoked the assembly of the disciples and said to them: " It is not fitting that the word of God should suffer because of our serving at table. Rather, let us choose seven brothers of good repute from among you, filled with the spirit and wisdom, and we will have them perform this service; as for us, let us remain in prayer and in the service of the word."

The disciples chose the best from among them. The Acts continue: " We presented them to the apostles, and after having prayed, they imposed their hands upon them." These were the deacons.

One sees, therefore, that the three orders of the hierarchy (the apostles, i.e., the bishops; the ancients, i.e., the priests; and the deacons) were established during the first days of the church's life. Each order had its particular function in achieving harmony for the total service of the community. This service extended to the spiritual needs as well as to the material cares of each and every one of the faithful.

Later, from the third to the fifth century, the church added to these three orders of divine institution the other less important orders: the subdiaconate, which is still a sacred and major order in the Latin Church, along with the four minor orders: acolyte, exorcist, lector, and porter. Each one performed his function according to the order that had been conferred upon him.

THE DIACONATE CONCEIVED AS AN INDEPENDENT FUNCTION

To study the diaconate more attentively, it is necessary to refer, above all, to the Code of Canon Law, where the functions exercised by the deacon are indicated. This order immediately precedes the reception of the priesthood. The Roman Pontifical enumerates three functions of the deacon in particular, which are also found in the Code: to distribute Holy Communion to the faithful, to baptize, and to preach.

Granted that the diaconate does not have a specific character today, for it constitutes only a necessary step to the priesthood, in practice, however, the Code demands for its reception all the spiritual, moral, and cultural dispositions that are required for ordination to the priesthood. Therefore, the same preparations and obligations as those of the priesthood are required, including celibacy and the breviary. In the Oriental Church, on the other hand, one can be admitted to the diaconate even after marriage.

It is premature to say what future course the Council will decide, based on today's discussion by the members of the Central Commission, concerning this schema prepared and presented by the Commission on the Discipline of the Sacraments. In any event, one can see that the great difficulties in the midst of which a large number of priests struggle, burdened by excessive pastoral work especially in the mission fields, have been well presented to the members of the Central Commission. These members are also familiar with the topics proposed during these past few years in international congresses. One in particular is to provide some well-prepared helpers for priests engaged in the pastoral care of souls, in all their secondary and time-consuming activities where their presence is dispensable.

Let us remember in relation to this question the words of Pius XII in his discourse of October 5, 1957, to the delegates of the Second International Congress of the Lay Apostolate: "We are thinking now of introducing an order of the diaconate, conceived as an ecclesiastical function independent of the priesthood. This idea, however, at least today, is not yet fully developed."

How has this idea developed during the past five years? How has it developed in its various forms and with the reservations that a complete vision of the problems would allow? It is the task of the Central Commission to answer these questions and in due time to make proposals on this subject.

THE RENEWAL OF THE MINOR ORDERS

The same can be said about the minor orders, i.e., certain ones could be revivified. Some could be reactivated in order to help priests in a more direct way, others to assist the faithful on a spiritual and a liturgical level, and still others to deal with the upkeep of buildings and sacred property. Today the care of these latter is often given to sacristans who are incapable or who are preoccupied with the problems of their own livelihood.

Finally, the initiatives that have been taken in the past few years (e.g., young lectors who held a diocesan congress in Rome these past few days, and whose first national congress is announced for next July) give us hope of happy results in the renewal of these institutions. These were created for specific ends, and could be usefully restored if they are given the modifications suggested by the experience of the centuries.

The more the Central Commission pursues its work, the more it gets into the urgent problems for the renewal of our Christian life. Respectful of tradition, and at the same time sensitive to the problems of the present, the Central Commission does not renounce anything of value from the past. Neither does it reject anything of value that the future might offer.

January 18, 1962

THE ORIENTAL CHURCHES

The agenda for this morning began regularly at nine thirty under the presidency of the dean, His Eminence Cardinal Tisserant. It continued in the same vein as yesterday with the report read at the end of the session on the questions concerning the Oriental Churches, by His Eminence Amleto Cardinal Cicognani, the secretary of state. This was done in his capacity as president of the Commission for the Oriental Churches.

Yesterday, the attention of the members and counselors of the Central Commission focused especially on the rites of the church. Today, pursuing the report of Cardinal Cicognani, the discussion turned to the Oriental patriarchs. We will try to give some explanation of each of these problems in order to enter better into the spirit of the future Council. We will also try to give some exact information regarding each problem submitted to the Preparatory Commission for examination.

THE DIVERSITY OF RITES IN THE CHURCH

In using the word " rite," we mean, above all, the way, the order or the rule, which is used in the celebration of sacred functions. By this word, we also understand the ceremonies, more or less solemn, of liturgical functions, and the celebration of religious feasts. The latter sense has been modified in part since January 1, 1961, by the new code of rubrics for the missal and the Roman breviary.

Finally, in a more exact sense, the term "rite" signifies the prescribed or habitual way of celebrating the liturgy. This usage of rites varies in certain territories of the church and among certain religious orders. A distinction also exists between Occidental and Oriental rites. Among Occidental rites known today, there are: the Roman rite, which is the most widespread in almost all of the Latin Church; the Ambrosian rite, used only in the diocese of Milan; and, in a more limited form, the Mozarabic rite, practiced for many centuries in Spain and preserved today only in the Chapel of Corpus Domini in Toledo; the Lyonnais rite, now almost completely assimilated to the Roman rite. These following rites have disappeared: the Gallican, the Celto-Irish, and a few others.

The rites proper to religious orders such as the Carthusians, Benedictines, Dominicans, and Carmelites are still in use with slight variations from the Roman rite.

The principal rites of the Oriental Church of our time are: the Alexandrian; the Antiochene, or Occidental Syriac; the Constantinopolitan, or Byzantine; the Chaldean, or Oriental Syriac; and the Armenian. Each one of these has its own branches with various names.

The Code of Canon Law protects and defends the individual rites, obliging the faithful to practice the rite in which they were baptized, forbidding priests to proselytize for the passage from one rite to another, and finally forbidding the transfer of rite without the approval of the Holy See. This means that the church considers all rites equal in dignity. There is nothing in itself that would prevent the development of new rites to satisfy the particular needs of a people and of particular religious situations.

The diversity of rites certainly in no way disrupts the unity of the church or its Catholic foundation. While safeguarding the principles of faith, morals, discipline, and obedience to the Roman Pontiff, the church respects all the traditions, customs, languages, and characteristics of each people in adapting herself to their needs. Moreover, the church takes it upon herself to inculcate in her priests and faithful of all rites the knowledge, respect, and a mutual esteem which are all essential factors for a deeper unity of faith and love in Christ.

THE DIGNITY OF ORIENTAL PATRIARCHS

First of all, let us enunciate this principle: concerning the power of jurisdiction, there are only two degrees in the sacred hierarchy by divine institution — the Supreme Pontiff, and the episcopacy which is subordinate to him. The patriarchs of the Oriental Church, recognized by tradition and by the Code as having an authority superior to that of bishops, consider their particular power of jurisdiction as purely ecclesiastical in origin, and consequently entirely under the authority of the Supreme Pontiff.

After this principle was reaffirmed, the Central Commission examined, with an all-embracing and fraternal spirit, the schema presented by His Eminence Amleto Cardinal Cicognani. This schema called for a recognition of the equality of the dignity of these patriarchs, in the external forum, either for the exercise of their powers or for their formal precedence. Their prestige is, in fact, linked to the historical heritage of their very ancient sees, a great number of which are of apostolic origin. These would be primarily the patriarchates of Constantinople, Alexandria, Egypt, Antioch, and Jerusalem. Their authority has been recognized since the first Councils of the church. In 325, the Council of Nicaea had already recognized the special supremacy of the bishops of Alexandria and Antioch. The Council of Constantinople, in 381, added to these the bishops of Constantinople, a city which had then become the capital of the Empire. The Council of Chalcedon, in 451, recognized equally the patriarchal powers of the

bishop of Jerusalem. With the passing of time, diverse patriarchates were created for particular rites. Today we still have
the patriarchates of Antioch for the Syrians, the Maronites,
and the Melkites; the patriarchate of Babylon for the Chaldeans; the patriarchate of Silicia for the Armenians; the patriarchate of Alexandria for the Copts. On the other hand, the
Latin patriarchate of Jerusalem is of rather recent origin.

THE LATIN PATRIARCHS

All that has been said here concerns only the Oriental Catholic patriarchs in communion with Rome and whose election
must be approved by the Supreme Pontiff. The more or less
titular patriarchs of the Latin Church have a different origin
and position. The patriarchate of Venice was derived from
the patriarchate of Aquila, dating back to the end of the sixth
century. The patriarchate of the West Indies, with his residence in Madrid, was created by Pope Leo X after the discovery of America. The patriarchate of Lisbon was granted by
Pope Clement VIII in 1716, and Patriarch of the East Indies
was the title given to the archbishop of Goa by Pope Leo XIII
in 1886.

January 19, 1962

LITURGY AND SACRAMENTS
IN ORIENTAL RITES

The meeting this morning can be considered as a natural
sequence of yesterday's meeting when Cardinal Cicognani
opened up the question of Oriental patriarchs. Again today,
the Cardinal Secretary of State, in his capacity as president of
the Commission for the Oriental Churches, read three reports:
the first concerned the relations of Catholics with non-Catholic Oriental Christians in the sacred ceremonies; the second
was on the use of vernacular languages in the Oriental liturgy;

and the third dealt with the sacraments in the Oriental Church. Thus progress is made in the study of these themes, which are interesting not only because of their historical aspects but also because of the influence that they can exert on Catholics themselves. For we repeat that the works of the Central Commission concerning the problems brought up by Cardinal Cicognani are uniquely concerned with Oriental Catholics, not with non-Catholics. This is true of all these questions: from the one on rites to the one on patriarchs, from those on sacred ceremonies to those on the liturgy and the sacraments. Given, however, the proximity of mentality, life, and religious costumes between Oriental Catholics and non-Catholics, these can trigger immediate repercussions of sympathy or of defiance among non-Catholics as well.

The Affinity in Sacred Functions
Between the Oriental Catholics and the Non-Catholics

The very fact that this subject was studied clearly shows the spirit of charity and fraternity that animates the preparation of the Council. There is no question here of any debate on the relationship with non-Catholic Orientals. Let us, however, remember the often-repeated counsel of the pope that we search for what unites rather than what divides. Except for the cases where true heresy or bad faith is present, there are numerous possibilities offered by modern life for meeting one another, for getting to know one another, for praying together fraternally to our same Father in heaven, and finally for esteeming and showing love for one another.

The road to unity is long and difficult. We do not destroy in one day the obstacles and prejudices that have built up over the centuries. But the first work to be done is precisely the one that the Central Commission indicates: to eliminate all the obstacles and possible misunderstandings without denying, of course, what is fundamental. The Lord cannot but bless every effort performed for this end.

The Use of Local Languages in the Oriental Liturgy

From time immemorial, the diverse Oriental liturgies have used a variety of languages. Language is not, obviously, an essential element in religious questions. A unique language certainly represents a solid factor for unity and an efficacious means of expressing truths more exactly. The church has always shown an understanding for the particular needs of Oriental Catholics, leaving to patriarchs and bishops the power to judge in each case the modifications to be made.

There is no question now of restricting such power, but of articulating it more solemnly at the occasion of the Council. And if the opportunity is given, this power could be broadened, having only the supreme end of the church in mind, which is to save souls and to clear the way for salvation.

The languages may be many; unique, however, is the heart that prays to God and unique the voice that rises to the Father, the voice of sons united in the same faith and the same love.

The Administration of the Sacraments

The members and counselors of the Central Commission have also studied the disciplinary aspects of three sacraments: Confirmation, Baptism, and Orders. But let us repeat that the question today concerns the administration of these sacraments in the Catholic Oriental Church, where customs are different from those of the Western Church. To the three sacraments mentioned above, Matrimony is added, especially to the extent that it concerns marriage between Catholic and Orthodox. Marriage in the Western Church will be treated in another session.

The Sacrament of Confirmation

We will add little to what we already said on Tuesday (January 16). Following a very ancient tradition in the Oriental Church, it is the priests themselves who administer Confirmation. On the other hand, according to the Councils of Florence and Trent, the ordinary minister of this sacrament is the bishop. A simple priest can only be its extraordinary minister.

This is why the Central Commission, in accord with its discussion on the administration of Confirmation in the Western Church, examined the opportuneness of continuing to administer Confirmation immediately after Baptism as do the Oriental priests. All the Oriental rites follow this ancient custom, with the exception of the Italo-Greek and the Maronite rites.

We have already emphasized that in the Western Church we should administer Confirmation before Holy Communion, not, however, during the early days of infancy. Concerning this question, an instruction of the Sacred Congregation of the Sacraments in 1932 stated that to give the sacrament of Confirmation before Communion " was opportune and more conformed to the nature and effects of the sacrament of Confirmation." The assembly of the French episcopacy, in 1952, made the same request, pointing out that it was more opportune not to postpone Confirmation beyond the seventh year.

January 20, 1962

THE INTEGRAL GUARD
OF THE DEPOSIT OF FAITH

The subjects of today's agenda, beginning the sixth meeting under the presidency of the dean, Eugene Cardinal Tisserant, are totally different from those subjects treated in the last sessions. The Theological Commission inaugurated, last Monday, January 15, the third session of the Central Commission. It opened with a report from its president, Alfredo Cardinal Ottaviani, on the moral order. The Commission also had the honor of closing this laborious week of studies and discussions by presenting its different schemata. The titles of these schemata can be grouped under one, which underlines the importance of the whole matter: the integral guarding of the deposit of faith.

Alfredo Cardinal Ottaviani, secretary of the Supreme Sacred Congregation of the Holy Office, briefly set forth the texts on the truth of faith in general, and God, the creator of the world. The members of the Central Commission then contributed their practical knowledge and experience acquired in the exercise of their most diverse pastoral ministries. As far as we are concerned, without divulging in any way the secret that surrounds the works of the Commission and its decisions, we would like to give some brief explanation on the subject in question. What do we understand by the " deposit of faith "? The word " deposit," taken in its juridical sense, means " the restoration of a good, not yet in full possession, but still under guard in order that it might be preserved integrally, to be given back at the opportune moment."

In our case, by the " deposit of faith " on the theological level, we understand all of divine revelation, contained in Holy Scripture and Tradition. This revelation is confided by God to his church, with a promise of special assistance from the Holy Spirit, so that no truth can be lost, deformed, or altered. This deposit of faith is indeed not a dead collection of documents, but on the contrary, a source of pure spring water, always gushing forth, and capable of quenching the thirst for truth that torments all men, wise or ignorant, everywhere and of all time. For this purpose, Jesus Christ entrusted the deposit of faith to Peter and his successors, so that by them and through them, it might be transmitted to all bishops of the church, defined by St. Paul as " the pillar and foundation of truth."

This is why the pope and the hierarchy united to him are the guardians, defenders, and natural administrators of the deposit of faith. In fact, let us repeat that to guard does not mean to hide or to bury, as the lazy servant of the parable did, but to vivify the presentation of the immutable truth, according to the needs of each time and mentality, and to progress in the knowledge of the truth contained in Scripture and Tradition. In this sense, the word "deposit," used by St. Paul in his first epistle to Timothy: "O Timothy, guard the deposit, avoid inane and irreligious discourses," and used by numerous fathers, has been a part of the terminology of Catholic theology since the sixteenth century, and has been, in a certain sense, ratified by the First Vatican Council.

HUMAN REASON AND THE TRUTHS OF FAITH

The church in her profound respect for the human intellect has always taught that man can arrive at the knowledge of God by reason. Pius XII in his encyclical *Humani generis* develops this subject in many ways, affirming that it is possible for man "to arrive at certain and immutable truth." Faith, which has revealed truth as object, is never opposed to reason, but rather enlightens and completes it by the presentation of truths that could not have been known without a special intervention of God through revelation. This does not prevent ignorance, the passions, and sin itself, however, from partially obscuring the human intellect, making it difficult to arrive at a knowledge of even those religious truths which are accessible to reason, for these truths are, by their very nature, often elevated and always delicate.

EXISTENTIALISM

We can mention here, without any pretense of deepening them, the theories of existentialism, which do not admit immutable truth. These theories affirm that truth is unstable and changes with the time, person, and situation, thereby transforming the objective realities into subjective phantasms. As far back as 1907, the Holy Office had condemned the doctrine according to which " truth changes, as man does, and evolves with him, in him, and by him." The encyclical *Humani generis* of 1950, already cited, condemned in turn the widespread philosophical system in the literature of the last decades which has been destroying the very bases of religion by denying the existence of constant truths and universal principles.

THE PROOFS FOR THE EXISTENCE OF GOD

It is necessary here to recall the fundamental truths of the catechism: Man was created to know, love, and serve God in this life, in order to see him and to rejoice with him in the next.

God, therefore, makes himself known to man, and in a certain sense, manifests himself to him by the works of his creation, which are like the mirrors of his existence and steps by which we ascend to him. The famous five proofs or five ways of St. Thomas for arriving at the knowledge of the existence of God are always valuable and effective. To these proofs, we can add those called " psychological," which are based on our need for happiness, love, justice, and truth. This need cannot remain eternally unsatisfied.

This precious and insistent reminder of the proofs for the existence of God is in itself a condemnation of atheism in all its forms. Atheism is even more reprehensible if it disguises itself under pseudoscientific appearances. This reminder is also a condemnation of all forms of pantheism as well, which tend to identify God with the world. Finally, it condemns all forms of deism that are more or less conscious, whereby one tends to empty God of all personal reality by mutilating his true nature and perfections, and attributing vague, subjective, and changing sentiments to him. The imagination here ultimately replaces reason, and reason rejects all faith.

ERRORS THAT HAVE DEVELOPED
SINCE THE LAST CENTURY

By reaffirming the fundamental truths of faith that proclaim God to be the principle and source of all life, the first cause of all movement and order, the creator of each man's soul, "made to His image and likeness," the schemata of the Theological Commission, presented today to the Central Commission, automatically reject the doctrine of material evolution as well as pantheistic and deistic evolution. These are obviously prominent themes of universal interest. It is true that the most diverse errors have attempted by fraud to infiltrate society through the centuries and even impose themselves by violence. But the vigilance of the church, even during the darkest hours of her history, has never weakened concerning the deposit of faith, which is her most sacred possession.

We gratefully look, then, with a comforted heart to the Holy Father and in his person to the bishops, who are so careful to keep intact the patrimony of truth entrusted to them by Christ. For these men are also desirous of seeking the best ways of making it available to souls through the turmoil of history.

Concerning the deposit of faith, the Second Council of the Vatican will change nothing that has already been established by Councils in the past. It will only confirm these past Councils and pursue its action along the same guideline, by denouncing the errors that have developed during the past century, by making particularly evident the most ignored and scorned truths, and by recalling those principles which will never undergo modification of any kind.

Thus it is that the Second Vatican Council in faithful obedience to the desire of the Holy Father, John XXIII, while remaining devoted to all that is living and immortal in the past, can bring about a mature renewal of faith, and a renovation of morals that will give new splendor to the image of the church.

January 22, 1962

REVELATION, DOGMAS, THE ORIGIN OF MAN

At this Monday meeting, the reports were again given by His Eminence Cardinal Ottaviani.

What do we understand by revelation?

The term "revelation," which comes from the Latin, means "to remove the veil," "to uncover," or "to manifest." In a theological sense, it indicates that manifestation by which God freely makes himself known to men.

God reveals himself first of all in his works and in all of nature. As the First Vatican Council said, this natural revelation consists in man's acquiring certain knowledge, through his own vision of creation, concerning the existence of God, and an obscure knowledge of God's nature and attributes.

But such was not the theme treated today by the Central Commission. It considered revelation properly so called, or supernatural revelation, i.e., the more direct manifestation that God made of himself to all men by the prophets and apostles, and above all by Jesus Christ, through the teaching of exalted truths that were unattainable by human reason alone. In his epistle to the Hebrews, St. Paul clearly says: "After having spoken many times and in diverse forms to our fathers by the prophets, God in these last days has spoken to us through his Son."

RATIONALISM AND MODERNISM

Along with the Pelagianism of old, in its denial of the need for divine revelation, errors against revelation have appeared again in more recent times in rationalism, which rejected in the name of reason the manifestations of truths superior to itself, and in modernism, which reduced revelation to a progressive natural and historical knowledge of divine things. What has been said thus far pertains only to the public revelation terminating with the apostolic period and given for all men.

PRIVATE REVELATION

We should speak separately on the subject of private revelations, which the church has admitted after long examination, proof, study, and experience. Concerning these, the church never tires of recommending prudence and extreme caution to the faithful, lest they become victims of mystification, personal or collective illusion, and of human or diabolical stratagems. Popes Benedict XIV, Pius X, Benedict XV, Pius XI, and Pius XII have given many previous directives on this point.

THE EVOLUTION OF DOGMA

Evolution of dogma is in no way contrary to the concept of revelation, as being definitive and complete with the death of the last apostle, John the Evangelist. What we call the evolution of dogma consists not in the numerical or qualitative change of dogmas but rather in the progressive knowledge we have of them by means of newer studies. The church guards in a vital way, as we have already said, the deposit of faith and benefits from the assistance of the Holy Spirit when she explores, interprets, or presents dogmas. She does not in any way increase, diminish, or transform them. There are not new truths, then, but truths of faith declared under the inspiration of the Holy Spirit. These truths have always been in the deposit of faith and then are presented in clearer light after centuries of study, after the research of many generations, and at times, after innumerable discussions.

THE NATURAL AND SUPERNATURAL ORDER

While treating the question of man's elevation from the natural to the supernatural order, the Central Commission took the opportunity to reexamine the fundamental truths which concern the end of man's creation, and grace which does not destroy but, rather, perfects man's nature. The elevation of man to the supernatural state was a gratuitous gift of God, and human nature had no right to share in it. The spiritual exigencies, moreover, in the soul made to the image of God lead us to consider the extreme value of such a gift, which was affirmed by St. Augustine, then by St. Thomas, and finally by the encyclical *Pascendi* of Pius X. Every theory that would claim a right to such an elevation or, on the other hand, would scorn it in the name of a false humanism would certainly be condemnable.

SPIRITISM

In the scope of this question, by means of contrast, are the problems, or rather the errors, of spiritism and of reincarnation, with all their derived forms of superstition — oracles, magic, sorcery, and horoscopes.

Spiritism, under its actual form of would-be communion with the spirits of the dead, has existed for little more than a hundred years. It was often condemned by the church because it endangered faith and morals. In 1856, even before the publication of the fundamental work on the doctrine of spiritism (the ferociously anti-Catholic work of Karder in 1869), the Holy Office solemnly declared the evocation of the dead to be illicit. This condemnation was renewed in diverse forms in 1882, 1897, 1898, and 1917, to cite only the best-known dates.

REINCARNATION

Closely related to spiritism is the theory of reincarnation in which certain ancient beliefs concerning metempsychosis are revived from paganism. It was explicitly condemned by the Second Council of Constantinople in 553. The Second Council of Lyons in 1274 and the Council of Florence in 1439 indirectly condemned the theory whereby a soul would pass from one human body to another, by affirming that the definitive judgment takes place immediately after death. But errors, like weeds, constantly arise, with slight variations and modern names designed to make them new and, therefore, more easily acceptable. But the vigilance of the church never allows itself to be abused, and thus reincarnation, under the false scientific appearances of theosophy, was condemned by the Holy Office in 1919.

ORIGINAL SIN AND MONOGENISM

By attempting, in our day, to exalt a new humanism, one admits with difficulty the idea of human nature being stained with original sin, and consequently weakened and corrupt. This is, however, a fundamental truth taught by the church, and is of interest in the domain of faith as well as in the domain of moral principles. In the study of all these aspects, the Central Commission clearly manifests that it sees modern man in his existential situation as menaced by snares and encircled by dangers.

Directly related to the doctrine of original sin is the doctrine of monogenism, that the unity of the human species derives its origin from only one man, Adam. On this point the church restricts herself to the teachings of St. Paul: " Just as by one man sin entered the world, and by sin death, so death has passed to all men from the fact that all have sinned." The Council of Trent and again the First Vatican Council explicitly recognized that the human race really descended from only one man. Furthermore, the encyclical *Humani generis* of Pius XII declares polygenism to be contrary to the very sources of revelation and unacceptable for a Catholic to believe.

These references which we have often made to preceding Councils show once again that the Second Vatican Council is directly linked with the whole conciliar tradition of the past, while, at the same time, it will represent a new step forward in the illumination of doctrine, the pointing out of equivocal and dangerous theories, and finally the eventual condemning of error.

January 23, 1962

THE BAPTISM OF THE NEWLY BORN AND SIN

This last session was again concerned with the reports of Cardinal Ottaviani.

The utility and even the necessity of baptizing infants as soon as possible so that, in case of death, they might obtain celestial beatitude or, if they live, they might be delivered from original sin and become the true children of God in the supernatural order, clearly appears in all the teaching of the fathers, doctors, preceding Councils, and Roman Pontiffs. Let us mention only Pius XII, who said in an allocution to a group of well-informed women in 1951: " In the present order, there is no other means [than Baptism] to communicate this [supernatural] life to the infant, who does not yet have the use of reason, for at the moment of death, the state of grace is necessary for salvation. Without this it is impossible to arrive at supernatural happiness and the beatific vision of God. An act of love can suffice for an adult to acquire sanctifying grace and to compensate for the absence of Baptism. This way is not open for the unborn or the newly born child."

Likewise the Code of Canon Law (canon 770) prescribes: " It is necessary to baptize the young infants as soon as possible." Pastors and preachers must frequently instruct the faithful on this serious duty incumbent upon them.

The second schema dealt with the question of reparation for the sins of men. The fact that Christ accomplished this by his own passion and death makes it especially obvious that sin is a true offense against God. For Jesus thereby satisfied the divine justice by vicariously assuming responsibility for all mankind.

The schema on the moral order, which was described on the first day of this January meeting, can be profitably recalled here. Modern disorder regarding the notion of good and evil was mentioned on that occasion. The tendency of denying any importance to sin or any responsibility before God is today no longer seen as a disorder but, rather, as the unavoidable fruit of surroundings, situations, nature, and, at times, of the subconscious itself. The fault, however, that required the reparation of the passion and death of the Son of God is, on the contrary, a serious matter.

FOURTH SESSION

DIOCESES AND EPISCOPAL CONFERENCES

In the Hall of the Congregations on the third floor of the Apostolic Palace, the fourth session of the Preparatory Central Commission of the Second Vatican Council opened this morning, February 20.

The Holy Father opened the meeting with a discourse in Latin, and then the Central Commission pursued its work under the presidency of Eugene Cardinal Tisserant. It discussed two schemata prepared by the Commission for Bishops and Diocesan Government, which were presented to the members and counselors of the Central Commission by Paolo Cardinal Marella. The first schema dealt with the actual situation of dioceses, and the second was on episcopal conferences.

THE LIFE AND DEVELOPMENT OF DIOCESES

The word " diocese," which is derived from a Greek term signifying " administration," means a well-defined territory over which a bishop exercises jurisdiction. The dioceses usually are named after the city in which the cathedral is situated and in which the bishop resides.

We can say that the institution of dioceses dates back to

apostolic times. In the course of their many missionary voyages, the apostles were careful to leave disciples (bishops) in the more important urban centers to head the new Christian communities founded by them. These disciples were surrounded by a college of ancients (priests) and deacons. The bishops were none other than the disciples of the apostles, whose work they continued after the deaths of the latter, and whose triple powers of teaching, ruling, and sanctifying a portion of the Christian people they inherited. These bishops inherited their powers by divine right and in virtue of their episcopal consecration.

At first, the limits of a diocese generally coincided with those of civil boundaries. Later, as a result of the extension of the faith and Christian life, appeals were made to the Roman Pontiff to constitute new dioceses having their own proper limits. In our day, according to Canon Law, the pope alone can create dioceses, when certain essential conditions are realized. He can suppress or reunite those which are too small or incapable of having their own autonomous life, and he can partition those which are too vast or overpopulated.

Concerning this subject, we must also mention the abbeys and prelatures nullius, which are territories that belong to no diocese and consequently depend on no bishop, whence the name nullius, i.e., " no one." The abbot or prelate, although a non-bishop, exercises an ordinary jurisdiction over the clergy and the people of the place under his authority.

At least three parishes are required for the erection of an abbey or prelature nullius. All that has thus far been said about dioceses applies as well with certain slight differences, noted in Canon Law, to the abbeys and prelatures nullius.

Precisely because of their ancient origin, dioceses have territories that do not always correspond to the new, practical exigencies of modern life. Some dioceses are too large, which makes it impossible for the bishop to know all his priests well, to visit all his parishes regularly, and to follow each important innovation. There are dioceses, on the other hand, that are too small, where the tempo of life is constantly decreasing. Works cannot flourish there because of a lack of space, means, and personnel, and the seminaries do not function as they should. There are some dioceses where the actual episcopal see is detached, almost isolated, in small centers, perhaps rich in historical and artistic heritage, but have now been surpassed in regard to population, road conditions, and civil importance by other more developed localities in these years of more intense commercial, tourist, and industrial life.

Such are the problems that the Commission for Bishops and Diocesan Government investigated and that the Central Commission examined today, keeping in mind the ends for which each diocese was constituted, i.e., to put the bishop who is the true pastor of the flock in the best position to know, love, and save his sheep.

Because of the speed characteristic of the modern world, it could be of great importance for obtaining these ends if the distances between the parishes and diocesan center were shortened. This would be done by transferring the episcopal see, as need be, and by better delineating the diocesan territory, i.e., by not encroaching on adjacent dioceses or isolating it from them.

The church is very prudent, and with good reason, when there is a question of changing that which has been established through centuries in order to answer the needs of the times. However, with equal consideration given, she can consider new situations and correct what would be an obstacle to the normal development of Christian life.

With all due regard for particular conditions, not only religious, but geographical, social, economic, and historical, the church cannot forget her mission, nor can she fail to seek constantly for the best means of accomplishing it, by adapting herself as far as possible to the new needs and conveniences of the faithful.

The importance of these questions examined today by the Central Commission certainly does not escape anyone who looks seriously at the life of the church which is called to live in the world and to make use of material means to accomplish her supernatural ends.

THE EPISCOPAL CONFERENCES

From the end of the last century, episcopal conferences have been founded in certain countries. These are periodic meetings of all the bishops of a country set up to discuss and study their common problems: either to study new forms and methods of the apostolate, capable of influencing the masses that have concentrated in large numbers, or to find a new line of defense against the better trained and organized adversaries. The ends of these conferences and their assemblies must be considered essentially pastoral, and they have shown themselves to be extremely useful in practice.

From Pius IX to John XXIII, the Supreme Pontiffs have all favored and often encouraged their establishment and development. Since 1898, Leo XIII in an instruction to an assembly of the bishops of the Austrian empire, indicated in twenty points the most relevant questions to be treated for the good of souls and the church. Then Pius XII, in an allocution to the cardinals and bishops in Rome for the proclamation of the liturgical feast of the Queenship of Mary, November, 1954, underlined in the following terms the importance of episcopal conferences: " To fulfill the pastoral office with fruit and efficacy, frequent relations between bishops are very useful. Thus we mutually help ourselves to acquire practical experience; we achieve a greater uniformity of government; we avoid the astonishment of the faithful who often do not understand why things are done one way in one diocese and differently or contrarily at times in the neighboring dioceses. The common meetings that have taken place almost everywhere are very useful for this purpose."

Each episcopal conference has its own proper statutes, approved by the Holy See, and which answer the particular needs of each country. These assemblies, which are not to be confused with plenary and provincial councils, study apostolic needs, and difficulties and dangers to souls, and deviations in the matter of faith and morals, as they arise from year to year. Special commissions are set up in these conferences to study more attentively fundamental problems such as Catholic organizations, catechism, and youth. Because we are progressing toward a society in which the particular characteristics of each people disappear through a leveling-off process, in which the problems and difficulties become almost the same for all, it is equally opportune that the bishops of different countries meet together, if not in international conferences, at least in councils where they can exchange, on a pastoral level, their experiences and ideas regarding their plans, initiatives, and projects. Let us mention in this matter, the Latin American Episcopal Council, whose see is at Bogotá, which brings together the delegates of the episcopal conferences of Latin America for reciprocal contact and collaboration.

In our day, these episcopal conferences of nations or of groups of nations, are regularly convoked. Some of these have already received approbation of their statutes, either definitively or on a trial basis. These are the conferences of: Argentina, Australia, Austria, Belgium, Bolivia, Brazil, British Antilles, Canada, Central America and Panama, Chile, Colombia, Congo, Cuba, Dominican Republic, Ecuador, El Salvador, France, French Africa, Germany, Great Britain, Guatemala, Haiti, India, Indonesia, Ireland, Italy, Japan, Korea, Mexico, Nigeria, Paraguay, Peru, Philippines, Poland, Portugal, Portuguese Africa, Ruanda-Urundi, South Africa, Spain, Switzerland, United States, Uruguay, Venezuela, and Yugoslavia.

The studies of the Central Commission, based on the schemata prepared by the particular commissions, face problems of vital and universal interest. We already find ourselves, in a certain sense, in a preconciliar climate.

February 21, 1962

THE RELATIONSHIP BETWEEN BISHOPS AND THE ROMAN CURIA; AND BISHOPS AND PASTORS

The Central Commission, presided over by the dean, Eugene Cardinal Tisserant, resumed its work this morning at nine thirty. It heard two other reports by Paolo Cardinal Marella, president of the Commission for Bishops and Diocesan Government, on the relations between bishops and the Roman Curia, on the one hand, and between bishops and pastors, on the other.

These subjects examined by the Central Commission flow naturally from those treated yesterday concerning dioceses and episcopal conferences.

In order to understand better the importance of these subjects, we will explain a few terms that pertain to them.

BISHOPS AND THE ROMAN CURIA

The bishop — from a Greek word meaning " to take care " — is by divine right the successor of the apostles. He governs with ordinary power, and under the authority of the Supreme Pontiff, a territory of the church, called a diocese. At the end of the first century St. Ignatius of Antioch said that in this function he was " the image of the Father," and St. Thomas designated the bishopric as the " spouse of the church."

The bishops are named by the pope, and their consecration is also reserved to him. The pope usually delegates this right to other bishops by apostolic mandate.

We distinguish residential bishops from titular bishops. The former are those who govern a real diocese; the latter have no real see or territory, but they are invested with the episcopal dignity of a see, which in earlier times was famous, but which now, sometimes even geographically, no longer exists.

The Roman Congregations "are stable commissions of cardinals to care for the affairs of the church." There are many cardinals in each congregation. One of them has the office of prefect, or the office of secretary if the authority of the prefect is reserved to the pope. This is the case, for instance, with the Holy Office, the Consistorial Congregation, and the Congregation for the Oriental Church. Each congregation concerns itself with matters relevant to it, as is, at times, indicated by its title.

The congregations were created as commissions to expedite administrative affairs when it was impossible for the Apostolic Chancery to deal with all the problems of the church. Their number and complexity have increased over the centuries. The first of these commissions was instituted by Paul III in 1542; then Pius IV, Gregory XIII, and Paul V instituted others. In their organic constitution, however, the congregations date back to Sixtus V in 1588. They remained as such with some modification up to the pontificate of Pius X, who promulgated the Constitution *Sapienti consilio* in 1908, thereby precisely determining the attributes of each congregation.

The relationship between the bishops and the Roman Curia certainly takes on great importance for the religious life of dioceses. It was in this context that Pius XII spoke to the cardinals and bishops united in Rome for the Marian year. Speaking of the necessity and frequency of these relations based on a mutual collaboration, he said: "To this reunion and to those relations among brothers in the episcopate must be added the frequent and vital meetings and relations with the Apostolic See. This habit of turning to the Holy See in what concerns, not only the faith, but also government and discipline, has been in force since the most ancient Christian times. . . . This union and these occasional contacts with the Holy See are not meant to reduce everything to unity, but are of divine right and proper to Christ's constitution of the church. Their result, far from hindering bishops, is, rather, to their advantage in the government of their own flock. These relations with the Holy See provide them with light and as-surance in doubtful questions; counsel and fortitude in dif-ficulties; help in hardships; and finally, comfort and consola-tion in critical situations. On the other hand, the Apostolic See derives from these relations with bishops a greater knowl-edge of the whole flock, more accurate and rapid knowledge of the dangers that threaten them and of remedies to be used to combat the dangers."

It is not only on account of motives which we call practical and pastoral that the necessity of these relations between bish-ops and Roman Congregations derives, but also from juridi-cal motives. The Roman Pontiff, by virtue of the primacy given him by Jesus Christ, can extend or limit episcopal juris-diction, which also comes immediately from Jesus Christ. By his power, which he uses exclusively for the unity and common good of the church, the Supreme Pontiff can reserve judg-ment on all major questions to himself, either because they are more important or because their solution is more difficult, or again because they concern major personalities.

This in no way implies that revision and change is impos-sible in these matters. Proposals have already been made along these lines at the First Vatican Council. The end envisaged was to obtain greater facility for bishops in the exercise of their rights and duties in governing their dioceses according to Canon Law, with legislative, judicial, and coercive powers as much on a spiritual as on the material plane.

Let us mention in this connection that there is a so-called quinquennial list of powers given to bishops, and renewable every five years, granted in answer to their wish to make the important affairs as easy to deal with as possible.

RELATIONS BETWEEN BISHOPS AND PASTORS

If the relations between bishops and the Roman Curia are essentially juridical, those between the bishops and the pas-tors, while also being juridical, must, however, be more like those between father and son, between master and disciple, and between superior and necessary, faithful collaborator.

The Roman Synod, in fact, states: " The parish is like the pivot of the diocese; around it, all the pastoral initiatives evolve, develop, and are ordered." The pastor is the heart and the soul and the mind of the parish.

The bishop certainly remains the father and shepherd of the flock of which the pastor himself is a member, but the pastor, as the Roman Synod states, named by the ecclesiastical authority, is also a true pastor and spiritual father, dependent on the bishop, whose son and collaborator he is.

This is why the pastor is more closely bound to his bishop than are the other priests. He consequently owes special obedience, fidelity, and respect in the exercise of all his affairs to the bishop.

The bishop, on the other hand, must know his pastors well, interest himself in their problems and difficulties, and follow their activities with solicitude and affection. Their works and priesthood have only one end — to save souls. This is why a bishop in naming a pastor chooses the best-fitted priest, also observing the dispositions of Canon Law, considering the spiritual, moral, and physical qualities that best correspond to the place, situations, needs, and persons of divers parishes.

We can here insert a problem that is often debated in priestly publications, i.e., the stability of pastors, actually sanctioned by Canon Law. One can hope for a greater facility in removing or changing a pastor who for divers motives, voluntary or not, no longer can effectively exercise his mission, all due precautions being observed in this matter.

The second day's work of the Central Commission closed with the discussion of problems of vast importance for the religious life of the faithful. The very fact that they were discussed is a sign of vitality in the church, which considers no accidental aspects as definitively acquired or immutable.

Paolo Cardinal Marella terminated this session with his reports on the studies of the Commission for Bishops and

Diocesan Government, over which he presides. We must admit the merit of this Commission's work in dealing with great questions of interest to the faithful themselves, even though they are not easily understood by the general public. We would be led to think that not all the problems studied are easily solved.

February 22, 1962

THE DUTIES OF PASTORS AND FAITHFUL

This morning, February 22, at ten thirty, immediately after the Holy Father's audience in the Basilica of St. Peter with all the resident clergy of Rome, the Central Commission met in the Hall of the Congregations to hear about and to discuss the two schemata presented by Pietro Cardinal Ciriaci, president of the Commission on the Discipline of the Clergy and the Christian People. The first was on the apostolic duties of pastors, and the second on the commandments of the church. These are two important questions for the pastoral ministry and the religious life of our time. The discourse that the Holy Father gave this morning to the cardinals, bishops, prelates, pastors, Lenten preachers, and clerics gathered in the Vatican Basilica dealt with themes that were later, by a happy coincidence, examined by the Central Commission for the preparation of the Council.

THE APOSTOLIC DUTIES OF PASTORS

Each pastor, as a direct collaborator with the bishop in the apostolate, fulfills the functions of master, priest, and shepherd.

As master, he must care for the catechetical formation of children, especially their preparation for the reception of the sacraments of Penance, Confirmation, and the Eucharist. He must preach the word of God on Sundays and on feast days. He must teach the value of the sacraments and the liturgical ceremonies at the occasion of baptisms, weddings, processions, funerals, and the blessing of homes.

The pastor must prepare himself for the serious and noble duties of master with a deep awareness of his responsibilities, with a sure knowledge of the doctrine that he must teach, with a broad spirit of adaptation to the needs of the souls, to their receptive capacities, to the exigencies of the times, and to the changing tastes of his audience. To present the truths in an attractive and modern manner is the ideal to which the pastor must strive. He must never surrender to the temptation of routine, of ready-made phrases, of superficiality, and of the pursuit of novelties.

He can find excellent collaborators, especially in the teaching of catechism, among the laity formed in Catholic associations, especially Catholic Action.

The pastor must take particular care of Catholic schools in places where non-Catholic or so-called neutral or mixed religious schools exist. The education that a child receives at school, if it is permeated with a secular or atheistic spirit, can at times render ineffective the religious catechetical formation that he receives.

As a priest, the pastor takes upon himself the task of having the whole religious life of the parish, without any distinction of persons, center around the sacrifice of the altar. A true liturgical education of the faithful is necessary so that they might participate ever more actively in the celebration of the sacred mysteries and so that they might nourish themselves ever more frequently with the Eucharist.

Here, as in preaching, the pastor must adapt the time and place of the services to the needs of the faithful, always remembering that he is at the service of souls. Modern times require a great spirit of adaptation in pastors, for these times offer great facility for mass travel and for leisure-time activities (sports, theater, and tourism) which are becoming available to all.

In his function as shepherd, the pastor has only one model,

the Good Shepherd, who knows each sheep, who guides all of them to the most wholesome pastures, who seeks the lost sheep, who cares for the sick, who forgives and seeks nothing for himself.

The pastor, who is at the same time meek and strong, is the man who knows neither threats nor dangers nor pains when the good of his parishioners is in question. He goes before them, performing spiritual and corporeal works of mercy. From the children he cares for at church, the youth he draws into sports activities and camps, the spouses he instructs in their new family duties, to the sick, the poor, and those rejected by all; from his faithful parishioners who surround him; from his resident parishioners to the transient faithful, there is no one whom the pastor must not love, care for, and save. Besides keeping his records in order, especially the one on the state of souls, of maintaining lively parish organizations, of performing his official duties with dignity, the pastor must also keep himself up to date on the most important problems, especially those of the church's life, in order to form his faithful with a Catholic and missionary spirit. Pastoral centers, sessions of adaptation, and meetings of the clergy can render great services in this matter.

The themes that the Central Commission studied today are exclusively pastoral. It is certain that the restoration and renewal of Christian faith and morals in our times depend upon their being practiced in the life of each parish.

THE COMMANDMENTS OF THE CHURCH

The Commission on the Discipline of the Clergy and the Christian People, after having prepared and presented diverse schemata on the life and duties of the priest (some last November and another today), in answer to its double title, was also interested in the duties of the Christian people, as the schema on the precepts of the church, discussed this morning, bears witness.

We all know from the catechism that besides the Ten Commandments of God, there are five commandments of the church, which bind in conscience under pain of serious sin. These are: the sanctification of Sundays and holy days, by assisting at Mass and abstaining from work; the Friday abstinence and fast on Ash Wednesday, Good Friday, the vigil of the Immaculate Conception, and the vigil of Christmas; the annual Confession and Communion, at least during Paschaltide, which starts on the first Sunday of Lent and ends on the Sunday after Pentecost; the contribution to the needs of the church; and the nonsolemn celebration of weddings during Advent and Lent.

In recent years, the church, in a desire to facilitate the fulfillment of certain precepts, has permitted the celebration of Mass at night, shortened the Eucharistic fast (three hours for solids and alcoholic beverages, and one hour for nonalcoholic beverages), transferred the day of fast to the vigil of the Immaculate Conception and the day of abstinence to the vigil of the Assumption, and abolished the obligation of fasting during all of Lent and the ember days, by reducing the obligation of fasting to four days only.

We must not think, however, that the obligation of prayer and penance no longer exists. The Council will certainly consider many modern exigencies, but it will not be able to abolish those forms of prayer and penance which the wisdom of the church has indicated as most useful from the earliest centuries. These have proved most helpful for the purification and sanctification of souls. We must not forget that the aim of the Council is to effect a renewal of religious life in the Christian people. This renewal cannot take place by rejecting all the prescriptions, or, what would be worse, by abolishing all that evoke the principles of mortification. If it is the aim of the Council to strengthen the spiritual values in a time when materialism and hedonism in general are widely rampant, it must recall the necessity of the commandments of the church. The Council will do this, however, by adapting them to the rhythm of modern life, if this is necessary, not so much to mitigate them as to facilitate their fulfillment.

This must be said in order to avoid useless illusion and disillusionment. Those who look on the Council from afar may tend to expect reform of an exterior sensational nature, forgetting that every true reform in the church always begins in the heart of man, in his soul and conscience.

Whatever conclusions the members and counselors of the Central Commission arrive at today, certainly the obligation of Mass and Sunday rest, of fast and abstinence on certain fixed and variable days according to the different situations in each country, of the annual Confession and Paschal Communion — these obligations will continue, at least in their substantial aspects. The times and exigencies change, but the human soul does not change and it must always follow the same roads to arrive at salvation.

February 23, 1962

RELIGIOUS

The work of the Central Commission began this morning, February 23, with the usual punctuality at nine thirty, under the presidency of the cardinal dean, Eugene Tisserant. The reports on the first two schemata, prepared by the Commission for Religious, were presented by Valerio Cardinal Valeri, president of the Commission. These following questions were examined: the lay religious congregations, the secular institutes, and religious vocations. On each one of these questions the members and counselors of the Central Commission gave their suggestions after each one had contributed his observation, experience, or proposition.

THE LAY RELIGIOUS CONGREGATIONS

We call lay congregations those religious institutes the majority of whose members have not received priestly ordination, although they live habitually in a community, with or without solemn vows. These congregations were born between the sixteenth and nineteenth centuries. Their aims, apart from the sanctification of the members, involve the works of charity and the apostolate, especially the education of youth.

One of the most evident signs of the constant vitality of the church is the continual blossoming of new forms of religious life which answer the special needs of people and times. The church can truly say that she is a fruitful and providential mother. She cares for the changing needs of men by favoring and consolidating the development of diverse religious families. These families really show, while remaining very close to the mentality and habits of the era in which they live, the highest ideals of the human soul: sanctity and the apostolate. Thus, through the most diverse periods of Christian civilization, the fervor of the religious life blossomed forth as vigorous trees nourishing themselves on the strength of well-determined historical epochs. Such are: the canons regular, the monastic and mendicant orders, the clerics regular, the clerical religious congregations, the societies of common life without vows, the lay religious congregations, and the secular institutes.

The schema presented this morning to the Central Commission underlined the importance of religious congregations that care for the instruction and education of youth. It did not, however, consider the problems of education as such. The matter in question is " a special vocation from God which must be cultivated and assisted with much care. Those who follow it give up the priesthood and its consolations," as Pius XII said. They do this in order to consecrate themselves wholeheartedly to teaching, not so much to the secular sciences as to Christian doctrine. One need only think of the importance and the value of the school where consciences are formed, and where not only the individuals but also the whole family and social community prepare for the future, in order to understand the great merit of those who consecrate themselves to this mission of forming the youth who represent all the hope of the church as well as of civil society according to Christian faith and morals. The instruction and education of youth have already been called by St. Gregory of Nazianzus fifteen centuries ago " the art of arts and the science of sciences." These words are always more true with the passing of time.

It is precisely because the mission of lay religious educators is difficult and delicate that they must adequately prepare themselves by theological studies which will allow them to teach the truths to be believed and the virtues to be practiced in an ever more clear, profound, and complete manner.

Let us mention only the following better known lay religious congregations founded for the Christian education of youth: the Brothers of the Christian Schools, founded in 1680 by St. John Baptist de la Salle, approved in 1725, having a present membership of 17,500; the Irish Christian Brothers, founded in 1802 by a layman, Edmund Rice, approved in 1820, which has a present enrollment of 3,500 members; the Marist Brothers, founded in 1817 by the Blessed Marcellin Champagnat and approved in 1867, with 9,000 members; the Sacred Heart Brothers, founded in 1821 by Rev. André Coindre and approved in 1894, with 3,000 members. Of the 27 lay religious congregations approved by the Holy See, about 20 have the instruction, education, and formation of the youth from all the social classes as their primary end.

SECULAR INSTITUTES

Side by side with the congregations and still more liberal in their form of life are the secular institutes. These are so called because their members wear no special habit, take no public vows, and maintain their social condition with all its practical and juridical consequences, even after their consecration to the Lord. Ecclesiastics as well as the laity can become members. They retain a certain liberty of movement, although bound by vows, for they do not follow a rule of common life, as is generally done in congregations and religious orders.

These institutes date back to the end of the eighteenth century. In 1889, the Sacred Congregation of bishops and regulars had already looked favorably on them, without, however, recognizing a true religious character in them. The Code of Canon Law made no mention of them; it waited until they arrived at a greater maturity.

It was on February 2, 1947, with the Constitution *Provida mater ecclesia,* that the secular institutes found their rightful place in the church. They contribute their youthful energies to the manifold needs and new forms of the apostolate in the modern world.

The secular institutes are clearly distinct from Catholic associations, although in them they often find a favorable milieu for the advent and development of their vocation. They are equally distinct from congregations and religious orders, which also pursue the ideal of Christian perfection by the practice of the three evangelical counsels.

Since they have a character all their own, they are also governed by the rules and statutes that are proper to them. Their witness is original, because they are the expression of a particular social and historical movement, and therefore they give an answer to a greater degree not only to modern man's way of thinking but also to his spiritual and moral needs.

The ends for which they have been created are extremely varied but they always answer the exigencies of a modern apostolate. The Society of St. Paul, founded in 1920, has as its purpose the bringing of true Christian life into society. The Opus Dei, founded in 1928, has as its purpose the diffusion of the principles of evangelical perfection to all classes, but especially to intellectuals. Others consecrate themselves to the formation of aspirants to the priesthood. They help diocesan priests practice the evangelical counsels while still being in and living in the world. The forms and methods are many, but the end is one: to have the ideal of a perfection, which has its immutable code in the gospel, shine forth in a modern world tending toward paganism.

THE VOCATION TO THE RELIGIOUS STATE

If there is a problem in regard to vocations to the priesthood, there is also a more serious problem in regard to a vocation to the religious state. Probably the cause is in the great difficulties which the religious state offers. Modern life, on the one hand so disorganized and confused, and on the other so rich in promise and attractions, unfortunately does not favor the advent and maturation of religious vocations.

Whatever the case may be, it is certain that God continues to call numerous souls to his love and service in our day as he did in the past. And it is also certain that his grace gives strength to numerous youth to renounce all in our day for a life of obedience, poverty, and chastity in the solitude of convents or in the fervor of the apostolate.

But given the difficulties that every aspirant to the religious life must surmount, it is necessary that a vocation be tested and nourished by a right intention. The reward for one's consecrating himself to His service is God alone, and not the human satisfactions that flow from a more or less quiet life or from posts of honor.

But when a vocation is sure, nothing must hinder its normal development in the best milieu, whatever the sacrifices might be which a definitive detachment imposes upon the youth who has been chosen by God, and upon his family. It is good to recall the Gospel: " Whoever has put his hand to the plow and looks back is not worthy of the Kingdom of God."

These are undoubtedly delicate problems which will not interest superficial people. It is, however, upon a proper solution of these problems — as well as the quest and defense of vocations examined today by the Central Commission — that, to a large extent, the restoration of the Christian life and the renewal of faith and morals depends. These are constantly referred to by the pope when he mentions the desired fruits hoped for from the forthcoming Council.

February 24, 1962

THE RELIGIOUS LIFE

This morning, February 24, again under the presidency of Eugene Cardinal Tisserant, the work of the Central Commission continued, with the examination of two other schemata prepared by the Commission for Religious, and presented by its president, Valerio Cardinal Valeri. They again considered the problems of religious life, the central importance of this life in the bosom of the church and also in civil society. Also considered were the opportuneness and necessity of always maintaining it at a high level of spirituality corresponding to the ideal of evangelical perfection, and the possibility of renewing the constitutions of congregations and the ancient orders in order to adapt them to the exigencies presented by the new media and techniques of modern life.

The fruitfulness of religious families and communities for men and women, from their manifold objectives which range from the apostolate in the most difficult milieus to the highest contemplation, not only manifests the perennial youth of the church, but is both a promise and an instrument of salvation for so many souls who need light and forgiveness. Needless to say, on the supernatural plane the value and fruitfulness of contemplation to which certain institutes of monastic life devote themselves are superior to all activity, even heroically generous works. We often say that the monasteries of strict observance are the lightning rods of a society that forgets God. This comparison is significant if we think of the evil that invades the world and of the necessity for some to pray, suffer, and intercede for all those who do not know how to pray, who seek pleasure even to the contempt of all law, and who, in a word, live as if God did not exist.

In order that the religious institutes, each one in its own specific domain, may again today attain the end intended by their founders, perhaps centuries ago, it may be necessary to return to its original spirit in the past in order to restore the full vigor of the rule, if this is necessary. And at the same time we must be solidly anchored in the present, adapting modes of life and action to the exigencies of times and places. This must be done without hindering in any way the ideal and spirit of the religious life in general and of each order and congregation in particular.

Our times impose on all those who glory in the name " Christian," and especially on those who walk in the way of perfection, the obligation of living in accord with the principles of their faith. It is therefore necessary for religious to enliven daily the fervor of their interior life, the spirit of sacrifice and of mortification, the practice of all the moral virtues, the perfect practice of obedience, chastity, and of individual and collective poverty, as far as is possible, and their detachment from the world. Anything that induces routine, quietude, tepidity, and mediocrity must be rejected from the heart by every religious, expelled from the monasteries, convents, and the institutes of all the orders and congregations.

Moreover, the exigencies of the apostolate as well as the lack of priests, and the ever-growing needs of the church in countries steeped in ancient Catholic customs that are in the process of dechristianization, as well as the mission countries, make another necessity evident, i.e., the need of greater unity for a more efficacious penetration into the modern world, and as a defense against the adversaries of the faith. If collaboration is strength, cooperation is a guarantee of success. For great enterprises can be dissipated and die if they remain isolated or refuse to unite with others, fearful of losing their own individuality.

It is well to recall here the discourse of Pius XII, dated December 9, 1957: " The ideal of religious perfection is one with the teachings of Christ and in particular with the evangelical counsels, and with his life, passion, and death. These are the inexhaustible springs where the heroism of every Christian generation is nourished. . . . They (the members of the state of perfection) must unite themselves with God by charity and offer themselves to him in holocaust; be consecrated to the service of Christ and his church, as active and chosen members of the mystical body. But once this essential obligation is well established, it is not forbidden them to think of renovation and its implementation. This must be done with true respect for tradition and without detracting from the proscriptions which the constitutions consider inviolable. Subordinates will observe that religious discipline which forbids them to take upon themselves what properly belongs to superiors and to undertake their own reforms which cannot be attempted without the authorization of their superiors."

And finally, Pius XII considered the delicate question of the interrelationship of different religious families in these words: " Let it suffice to recall that while preserving the existing and necessary distinctions between the communities, we must tend to unite and collaborate with sincerity and goodwill. There exists, in fact, a kind of common good of communities, which supposes that each one is ready to consider the others, and to adapt itself to the exigencies of a coordination that necessarily entails some self-denial for the common good."

The continual invitations of Pope John XXIII to the restoring, renewing, and updating of Christian life are equally valid for the restoration, renewal, and updating of religious life, without fear of exaggeration and without prejudice to anyone.

Valerio Cardinal Valeri ended his report on the subjects relevant to the Commission over which he presides. These subjects were the order of the day for this fourth session. The first week's work thus came to a close with these important questions. Thus, during the first week's work, in spite of the loss of a day, ten schemata were examined in five days, averaging two schemata a day. The Holy Father, in his opening discourse, announced a hardworking session. We can say that it was not only hardworking but also fruitful in good results.

The floor was then given to Cardinal Pizzardo.

VOCATIONS

Already last Saturday at the end of the session, as we have announced, the members and counselors of the Central Commission listened to a report by Giuseppe Cardinal Pizzardo, president of the Commission on Studies and Seminaries. It examined a schema on ecclesiastical vocations.

This is certainly one of the most vital and difficult problems, dear to the heart of the Holy Father and many pastors of dioceses. The situation already expressed by Jesus to his apostles in this striking image: "The harvest is great but the laborers are few," has certainly not improved through the centuries.

The situation even becomes more critical in our times for many reasons. And the voice of the Supreme Pontiffs has been heard often in these past decades, repeating the invitation of the Master: "Pray that the Lord send workers to the harvest."

Recent statistics show that situations are different from country to country. While there is on the average 1 priest for 1,100 Catholics in Europe, there is 1 for about 12,000 Catholics in Latin America. There are 228,000 priests and 418,000,000 Catholics in the 1,100 dioceses in communion with the Sacred Congregation of Seminaries. This, then, is roughly 1 priest for every 1,500 faithful, but we would need 200,000 priests more to answer the needs of Catholics alone without considering the mission countries. In these mission lands, it is difficult to establish statistics, for the needs are really incalculable.

The problem is equally felt in Italy, especially in certain regions. In 1960, there were 51 new priests more than in 1959;

but there were also 86 more deceased priests. We must consider, moreover, always limiting ourselves to the problem of Italy, that over 10,000 priests of the 43,000 actually living are over sixty years of age. In the light of these figures, however incomplete they may be, we see that the need for vocations is so urgent that it demands the cooperation of all in order that the great gaps in the apostolate may be filled.

No one can turn his back on this problem if he considers himself a sincere son of the church: from the bishops, who have the pastoral responsibilities and face the ever-growing needs of souls, to the youth who experience the attractions of the priesthood; from priests to parents, and from educators to the diverse members of Catholic organizations. Pius XII affirmed: " It is a fact that the number of priestly vocations is not the only norm but one of the most sure norms to measure the value of a Catholic school, as well as other establishments of education. This is also true in measuring its fruitfulness, not only in the ecclesiastical ministry but also in every domain of lay activity."

All means must be used, and above all, prayer, which is the most efficacious and always at hand for all people of goodwill. Other means to be used include: the religious instruction of children and adults — the formation of youth and the preparation of spouses for their task of education; the place given in the press to questions concerning the church, especially where there is a lack of priests; aid for seminaries; the organization in every diocese of the work for ecclesiastical vocations, instituted by the *motu proprio Eum nobis* in 1941, and developed in these latter years. During the first Congress for Ecclesiastical Vocations in 1961, the Holy Father said: " Our concern is for all the nations of the world, especially those of Latin America, where the vast territories and the rapid population growth, among other reasons, have made the solution of this vocation problem difficult."

Here is how John XXIII expresses himself on this question: " The problem of ecclesiastical and religious vocations is the daily concern of the pope, the breath of his prayer, and the ardent aspiration of his soul."

February 26, 1962

SEMINARIES

This morning, February 26, the Central Commission pursued its work by examining the schemata that were closely related to the preceding one on vocations. Giuseppe Cardinal Pizzardo again reported.

In order that a vocation might arrive at complete maturity, it must be cultivated for many years in seminaries. These special colleges are established to give a spiritual and ascetic formation to the young aspirant for the priesthood, in order to prepare him by the use of a wide curriculum of studies ranging from the sciences and the letters, as a basis for his humanistic preparation, to philosophy and the different branches of ecclesiastical science, e.g., Holy Scripture, dogmatic and moral theology, Canon Law, pastoral theology and patrology, liturgy and ecclesiastical history. All these subjects must be taught not only by competent masters in each discipline but in a complete and harmonious manner in order to offer the students a panoramic vision and to form in them a whole unity of knowledge that complements itself. Nothing is more conducive to a superficial mind than fragmentary isolated bits of knowledge which necessarily remain incomplete.

Learning has only one end: to prepare cultured priests in the necessary sacred sciences so they can express and exercise their pastoral ministry with dignity and competence, possessing at the same time a universal vision of even the most recent problems in the church — the missions, the lay apostolate, the unity of Christians, and the media of public communications.

If because of a lack of sufficient students or competent teachers in the different subjects, it would be deemed necessary to risk an inadequate formation for the priestly mission and needs of the times, we could then study the possibility of uniting students from different ecclesiastical localities into interdiocesan seminaries. The program of studies also could be adapted to answer local needs better on a national level by the bishops of each country. All these bishops, however, must keep the general rules of the Holy See in mind.

The church has always cared for the spiritual and cultural formation of her priests, and many colleges were established for this purpose. It was the Council of Trent in 1563 that decreed the formation of a perpetual seminary in each diocese. Here, the bishop could religiously nourish, educate, and form the young aspirants to the priesthood in the sacred disciplines. The following year, in 1564, St. Charles Borromeo had already begun the first seminary; others immediately followed in Rome, Italy, and in many nations of Europe.

These seminaries had a vast influence in the seventeenth century, thanks also to the example of St. Gregory Barbarigo, who made an exemplary institution of the seminary of Padua.

Later St. Pius X instituted the regional seminaries of Italy, which were then strengthened by Pius XI. There is a wealth of legislation, doctrine, exhortation, and practical advice concerning the spiritual formation and the sacred learning to be given in seminaries in these following documents: *Haerent animo* — Pius X; *Ad Catholici sacerdotii* — Pius XI; *Humani generis* — Pius XII; *Menti nostrae* — Pius XII; *Sacerdotii nostri primordia* — John XXIII; and in many other allocutions on the priesthood and the preparation for it by Pope John XXIII.

ECCLESIASTICAL UNIVERSITIES

What was said about seminaries applies equally to the universities of the church. These are called to play an ever-greater role in the formation of those who will in turn teach in seminaries and religious institutions, after they receive their academic degrees.

The Apostolic Constitution of Pius XI, *Deus scientiarum* of May 24, 1931, indicates the exalted ends for which these universities were established. The sacred sciences would not only be taught in these but also cultivated, enriched, and deepened. Universities also face the problems of specialization, e.g., patrology, history of religion, missiology, Christian archaeology, sacred art, the science of Catholic confessions, the social sciences, the ethnological and anthropological sciences, journalism and the modern media of social communications (radio, cinema, and television).

Let us mention the ecclesiastical universities and athenaeums in Rome at the present time: the Pontifical Gregorian University, whose origins date back to 1652 and which is directed by the Society of Jesus; the Pontifical Lateran University, founded as an athenaeum in 1824 by Leo XII and given the title of Pontifical University in 1959; the Urban Pontifical Athenaeum *De propaganda fide,* founded in 1627 by Urban VIII; the Pontifical Athenaeum *Angelicum,* established in 1580 as a college for the Dominican students and conferring academic degrees equally on other students in 1727, and becoming an international pontifical institute in 1909; the Pontifical Athenaeum of St. Anselm, founded in 1687 for the Benedictines by Innocent XI and becoming pontifical in 1933; the Antonine Pontifical Athenaeum, erected in 1933 and becoming pontifical in 1938; the Salesian Pontifical Athenaeum, founded in 1940; the Pontifical Institute of Sacred Music, founded by Pius X in 1911. There is also the pontifical faculty of theology of St. Bonaventure, of the Friars Minor Conventuals, whose origin dates back to 1587, which was reconfirmed in 1933 and became pontifical in 1955; the theological faculty of the Discalced Carmelites, instituted in 1935; the Marian theological faculty of the Servites of Mary, established in 1666, and instituted *in perpetuum* in 1955.

The church has other universities and athenaeums in the world. Some are very ancient and have a worldwide reputation.

February 27, 1962

CATHOLIC UNIVERSITIES

This morning, February 27, at nine thirty, under the presidency of Eugene Cardinal Tisserant, the Central Commission opened its last meeting of the fourth session. The Holy Father came in at the end of the work to conclude these laborious and important meetings with an address.

Giuseppe Cardinal Pizzardo, continuing the presentation of the schemata prepared by the Commission on Studies and Seminaries over which he presides, developed the question of Catholic universities. Ample discussion followed the presentation of this subject.

The Latin word *universitas* — which signifies " totality," " universality " — was used in the Middle Ages to designate the corporations of the different arts and crafts. It continued to designate the advanced schools when, at the end of the twelfth century, the student corporation of Bologna affirmed itself and acquired a special notability. This word designated either the place and the establishment of general study, open to all students, or the corporation of students and the professors who regulated the institutions of learning. Each protected its own interests.

Today a university represents the summit of all learning. It crowns the cycle of studies in the specialized faculties of every discipline and confers academic degrees.

Everyone knows that the first universities were desired, instituted, and often directed, by the church. The Abbey of Monte Cassino contributed greatly to the first and perhaps the most famous, the University of Salerno, established in the middle of the eleventh century. This university was born gradually from the development of ecclesiastical schools which united the students from all the European countries. The University of Paris, on the other hand, originated from the Cathedral School of Notre Dame. Its definitive statutes were approved in 1231. The Universities of Oxford and Cambridge were made famous by their Franciscan and Dominican masters.

Very soon other universities sprang up in almost every country in Europe, modeling themselves on those already existing. The Universities of Padua, Toulouse, Salamanca, Vienna, Leipzig, Louvain, Prague, and of Kraków, all instituted from the twelfth to the fifteenth century, became particularly famous.

Addressing himself to Catholic students in 1941, Pius XII said: " The universities and athenaeums are neither of today nor of yesterday; they were born in the Middle Ages, in the bosom of and under the protection of the church. Even then one finds errors, heresies, and antisocial theories. At that time, however, thanks to the universities that formed and directed the minds, the general atmosphere was impregnated with Christian concepts. One saw the light of this faith shine forth, this faith which does not minimize talents but rather makes them greater, seeing them as reflections of God. This concept is often discredited today."

With the advent of humanism and then the Reformation, universities lost almost all their original sacred character; and after they had removed theology from their program, they often became centers where science and the arts opposed faith. Thus we have the constant preoccupation of the church to establish her own Catholic universities. Let us mention only the Universities of Mexico and Lima, founded in 1555, a little over sixty years after the discovery of the New World. The University of Louvain, founded by Martin V in 1425, was reconstituted by the bishops of Belgium in 1833, with the approval of Gregory XVI.

We count today 37 Catholic universities with over 150,000 students in the world. These are: Léopoldville in the Congo, founded in 1957; Tokyo, Japan (1913) ; Beirut, Lebanon (1881) ; Manila, Philippines (1645) ; thirteen were founded in Europe at different times: Louvain, Belgium (1425) ; Angers

(1877), Lille (1876), Lyons (1886), Paris (1875), Toulouse (1889), France; Milan, Italy (1920); Maynooth, Ireland (1896); Nimeguen, Holland (1923); Lublin, Poland (1920); Comillas (1904), Salamanca (1940), Pamplona (1960), Spain.

There are thirteen others in Latin America: Buenos Aires, Argentina (1960); São Paulo (1947), Rio de Janeiro (1947), Pôrto Alegre (1950), Campinas (1956), Brazil; Central America: Havana, Cuba (1957); Santiago (1930), Valparaíso (1961), Chile; Bogotá (1937), Medellín (1945), Colombia; Quito (1954), Ecuador; Lima (1555), Peru, this primitive university has been restored.

North America has 7 Catholic universities: 4 in Canada, and 3 in the United States. The Canadian universities are: Quebec (1876), Ottawa (1889), Montreal (1927), and Sherbrooke (1957). Those in the United States are: Washington (1889), Niagara Falls (1956), Chicago (1957).

There are 27 state universities in 11 European countries with theological faculties. Some of them have unfortunately been suppressed in Communist-dominated countries.

We can name, moreover, 3 faculties for the formation of professors: one in Castelnuova Fogliani, near Piacenza; another in Rome, reserved for religious; and the third at Asmara, in Eritrea.

Almost all the Catholic universities were federated in 1924. This federation was disrupted during the war and reestablished in 1949.

The importance and purposes of Catholic universities have been amply developed in the Apostolic Constitution *Deus scientiarum Dominus,* of Pius XI. Pius XII has also insisted on the indispensable function of Catholic universities, in speaking to elite groups from different countries. To the directors, professors, and students of the French Catholic institutes, he said: " The permanent function of Catholic institutes or universities resides in their usefulness for setting up a well-ordered and solid body of doctrine and for creating a whole cultural atmosphere that is specifically Catholic. Even the most laudable learning in every branch of knowledge complemented by a superior religious instruction does not suffice. All the sciences have some direct or indirect relation to religion, not only theology, philosophy, history, and literature, but also the other sciences: law, medicine, physics, cosmology, paleontology, philology. . . . Even if the learning itself is not directly concerned with the religious truth and conscience, it must nonetheless be permeated with the Catholic religion."

From this we can clearly see the Central Commission's motive in this important question. The preparing of professors for an ever-higher level of teaching, the encouraging of students to have them choose Catholic universities where sciences are taught in the light of faith, and the inviting of Catholics to support their universities from which better formed Catholic laity come — all these constitute fundamental questions that cannot be ignored by the church.

THE CHURCH'S PRESCRIPTION
FOR CATHOLICS OF ORIENTAL RITES

Immediately after the discussion on Catholic universities, Giovani Amleto Cardinal Cicognani presented the prescriptions of the church concerning the Catholics of Oriental rites.

There is not much to be added to what was said a few days ago on this subject, presented in the schema prepared by the Commission on the Discipline of the Clergy and the Christian People. The precepts of prayer and Sunday rest, of penance and in particular the Lenten fast and abstinence, of the Paschal Communion and the support of the church according to each one's ability, and the prohibition of weddings during Advent and Lent — all these precepts are valid for the faithful of any rite. Different customs and traditions, however, as well as the particular dispositions of the Oriental patriarchs and bishops, according to the needs of their dioceses and the prescriptions of each rite, must be kept in mind.

The works of this fourth session came to an end, but other

schemata will be examined by the members of the Central Commission. These members are about to leave today and tomorrow for their respective sees. The study of these schemata then will be possible before the next session on March 26.

FIFTH SESSION

March 26, 1962

LITURGY

Yesterday morning, Monday, the work of the fifth session of the Central Commission got under way. There were 63 members and 16 advisers participating.

L'Osservatore Romano listed as present 20 cardinals of the Curia, 22 residential cardinal archbishops, 1 patriarch, 14 archbishops, 3 bishops, and 3 superior generals of religious orders.

The question of the day was the liturgy, presented in its broad lines by the president of the Liturgical Commission, Arcadio Cardinal Larraona, who is also the prefect of the Congregation of Rites.

The word " liturgy," which comes from the Greek, signifies work, service, or public office performed in the interest of all. Since the beginning of Christianity, as in the Old Law, this word has signified the sacred acts performed by the priests in the name of the faithful for the worship of God.

The liturgy can be defined more simply and briefly as the worship given to God by the church; or in a more complete way, " The Holy liturgy is the public worship that our Redeemer gives to the Father as the Head of the church; it is also the worship given by the society of the faithful to its head and by him to the eternal Father; it is, in a word, the integral worship of the mystical body of Christ, that is to say, of the Head and his members."

This definition is taken from the encyclical *Mediator Dei* of Pius XII, dated November 20, 1947. This document of primary importance encourages the modern liturgical movement, and analyzes precisely the exaggerated and sometimes erroneous tendencies in the liturgical sphere.

This encyclical also gives the fundamental principles on the nature of the liturgy and the place it should hold in the life of the church and of each member.

The liturgy, however, is not the whole activity of the church. This activity is also expressed in multiple teaching, governing, and apostolic functions. But for the whole activity of the church, the liturgy is the source from which grace is born and the end toward which souls tend. Consequently, without condemning or rejecting forms of individual piety that are approved by ecclesiastical authority and can be useful means of sanctification, we must give the first place to liturgical prayer. The instruction of the Sacred Congregation of Rites on the new liturgical order for Holy Week explicitly exhorts "to instruct the faithful in the great value of the sacred liturgy, which from its nature always surpasses all the other customs and devotions, as excellent as they may be."

THE PRINCIPLES FOR LITURGICAL REFORM

Hence there is the necessity always to favor, in the seminaries and religious institutes, formation in true liturgical piety, in order that the faithful may in turn learn to love, understand, and live the liturgy. There is much talk and writing on the liturgy today. This is certainly useful and laudable. There are some also who propose this or that reform. On this point, we must keep two observations in mind from the encyclical *Mediator Dei*. The first says: " Since the sacred liturgy is performed in the first place by the priests in the name of the church, its order, regulations, and form must depend on the authority of the church. This principle which flows from the very nature of Christian worship, is confirmed by the documents of history." The Code of Canon Law says likewise: " The ordering of the liturgy and the approbation of the liturgical books belong to the Apostolic See and to it alone."

The Code underlines that " the sacred liturgy is formed of human and divine elements; of course the latter, established by the Divine Redeemer, can in no way be changed by men. The former, however, can undergo diverse modifications according to the demands of the times, and of souls insofar as the ecclesiastical hierarchy helped by the Holy Spirit will have approved them."

THE LITURGICAL BOOKS

The decree of the Sacred Congregation of Rites on May 17, 1911, said that for the Western Church of the Latin rite " the main liturgical books are: the missal, the breviary, the pontifical, the martyrology, the ceremonial of bishops, the propers of Masses, and the offices for certain dioceses or religious orders, the memorial of rites of Benedict XIII for the small churches, the Clementine instruction for the exposition of the Blessed Sacrament during the forty hours and the collection of decrees of the Sacred Congregation of Rites."

There are two editions of liturgical books: the typical edition and the one conformed to the typical edition. No liturgical book can be printed without the authorization of the Sacred Congregation of Rites. The Holy See, furthermore, reserves to itself all property rights to the editions of the liturgical books.

The language used in liturgical books in the Western Church is exclusively Latin. In the Oriental Church, on the other hand, many other languages are used.

THE LITURGICAL MOVEMENT

The first decades of the last century saw the beginnings of the liturgical movement which proposed " to make live again the better traditions of Canon Law and those of the liturgy which had fallen into decadence." This movement found the environment needed for development especially in certain Benedictine monasteries. It then spread rapidly from Europe to the entire world. The movement received a new impetus from St. Pius X. Centers of liturgical activity were created. Their main objective was that of encouraging the active participation of the faithful in the liturgy and in a deeper study of the liturgy in its true dogmatic and ascetical content. Pius XII, in a brief synthesis, outlined the major phases of the liturgical movement over the past sixty years: " If we compare the actual situation of the liturgical movement with what it was thirty years ago, we see that it has made undeniable progress in extension as well as depth. . . . The main impetus in the doctrine as well as in the practical application came from the hierarchy and in particular from our holy predecessor, Pius X. By his *motu proprio Abhinc duos annos* of October 23, 1913, he gave a decisive impetus to the liturgical movement."

March 27, 1962

THE ACTIVE PARTICIPATION
OF THE FAITHFUL AT MASS

The work of the Central Commission continued this morning still under the presidency of Cardinal Tisserant. The first subject treated was the liturgy. During the second part of yesterday's meeting, Arcadio Cardinal Larraona presented the second chapter of the schema on the Holy Eucharistic mystery, i.e., the Mass. This morning a discussion followed and a vote was taken on the schema.

Then the Central Commission considered a few schemata on the missions presented by Gregory Peter Cardinal Agagianian, the patriarch of Silicia for the Armenians, the president of the Commission on the Missions, and prefect of the Congregation for the Propagation of the Faith.

To the members present yesterday, these were added today: Cardinals Traglia, Valeri, Frings, Agagianian; Msgr. Alberto Gori, patriarch of Jerusalem; Msgr. Yago, archbishop of Abidjan; and Msgr. Lefebvre, bishop of Tulle.

At the center of all the liturgy, there is the sacrifice of the Mass. The encyclical *Mediator Dei* of Pius XII defines the mystery of the Holy Eucharist in these words: " It is the culminating point and the center of the Christian religion." It is therefore necessary that the faithful truly assist at the celebration of the Eucharistic mystery and not sit as though they were mute and passive spectators, as they often do. They must actively take part in it by understanding well the rites and prayers, by responding to the Spirit, by offering themselves with the host and the wine offered by the priest, by nourishing their minds with the truths taught in Holy Scripture, and by revitalizing their souls with Communion received as often as possible along with the priest's own Communion.

A MORE ATTENTIVE CHOICE OF SCRIPTURAL TEXTS TO BE USED AT MASS

In order that there may be an ever more conscious and devoted attitude among the greatest possible number of the faithful, formation adapted to the intelligence and devotion of all Christians is necessary. Also, a revision will be useful. This revision will more greatly emphasize the nature and significance of the words, gestures, and rites, while keeping intact the actual order of the Mass. The current liturgical movement, with its studies on the origin and evolution of the various parts of the Mass, has certainly brought about a more precise knowledge of the parts added over the course of centuries.

These added parts have often made the primitive rites cumbersome. A more attentive choice of the Scriptural texts in the first part of the liturgy of the Mass, i.e., the part of the catechumens that is essentially doctrinal and didactic, could help the faithful to unite themselves more intimately with the celebrant in the second part of the liturgy, i.e., the part called the Eucharistic sacrifice. Cardinal Schuster, who knows liturgical and pastoral problems well, Cardinal Faulhaber, and others have already underlined the usefulness of proposing to the meditation of the faithful, in the framework of the annual liturgical cycle, a better and greater choice of lessons taken from Holy Scripture. These lessons contain hidden treasures which few people know because they appear in no part or cycle of the liturgy. The homily itself, i.e., the explanation of the Gospel, could profitably become a part of the " liturgy of the word " during the Mass, especially on feast days, rather than being a more or less marginal appendix.

Other chapters of the same schema on the liturgy will be examined, always in a rigorous perspective of equilibrium between the present and the past, by the Central Commission in the next few days.

" The liturgy," said Pius XII, " confers to the life of the church and to the whole religious attitude of our day a characteristic mark." These preparatory studies of the Council have been pursued in order that this characteristic mark might be ever more beneficial and so that the faithful might take a more active and conscious part in the liturgical action.

March 30, 1962

THE SACRAMENTS

The Central Commission, still under the presidency of Cardinal Tisserant, treated today, March 30, the problems of the liturgy. The chairman was Cardinal Larraona. In the second part of yesterday's session, the third chapter of the liturgy treating of sacraments and sacramentals, had already been examined.

The sacraments, instituted by Jesus Christ, are the sensible and efficacious signs of grace. The whole liturgy is a sign, a manifestation of the truth and of the Christian mysteries. These sacraments indicate an invisible reality under symbolic form. They produce and increase this reality which they signify. Only God, in fact, can cause the spiritual supernatural effect of grace to be produced by means of material elements such as bread, water, etc.

The Code says in canons 731 and 733: " The sacraments of the New Law, being the principal means of sanctity and salvation, must be administered and received with great devotion and respect, in conformity with the prescribed ceremonies of the liturgical books."

It is this aspect of the sacraments which particularly interested the Central Commission yesterday, and not the doctrinal aspects. For these latter we have the definitions of the Council of Trent contained in the thirteen canons of the seventh session, and the condemnation of the errors of modernism by Pius X in 1907.

Around the essential rite of each sacrament, many ceremonies have developed over the course of the centuries; their end was to make evident the importance of the sacrament. It was the intelligibility and significance of these ceremonies which held the attention of the Central Commission.

THE SACRAMENTALS

Canon 1144 defines the nature of sacramentals: " They are certain rites, actions, or objects used by the church in imitation of the sacraments to obtain by their intercession certain effects especially of a spiritual order."

Sacramentals are different from sacraments in many ways. They are of ecclesiastical institution. They also do not produce grace but obtain by the church's intercession particular graces, i.e., spiritual favors. They have no efficacy of themselves but only by the intercession of the church. They vary in number as canon 1145 states: " Only the Holy See can create new sacramentals and suppress, modify, and authentically interpret those already existing."

The sacramentals are numerous: prayer in general, and in particular the Our Father and public prayers, the signs of the cross, the aspirations with holy water, unctions, consecrations, blessed food, the recitation of the Confiteor and other acts of humility, alms and other works of mercy, and the multiple blessings of objects and persons.

The liturgical book that contains the formulas and rubrics of sacramentals as well as the rites of the sacraments is the Ritual. Its first official publication dates from Paul V in 1614. It contains the sacraments that a priest can give, the chants and prayers of liturgical processions, the rites of funerals, the formulas of the benedictions that can be given by a priest, and the formula of exorcisms.

There were certain parts of the Ritual, then, which were examined by the Central Commission yesterday.

Today, Cardinal Larraona presented the fourth and fifth chapters of the liturgy, devoted to the divine office and the liturgical year.

THE DIVINE OFFICE

In the encyclical *Mediator Dei* of Pius XII, the divine office is defined as " the prayer of the mystical body of Christ addressed to God, in the name of and for the advantage of all Christians by the priest and the other ministers of the church, as well as by the religious delegated by her to secure this effect."

The divine office, then, is the same prayer of Jesus continued through the centuries by his priests.

Usually, in speaking of the divine office, we use the word " breviary," i.e., the container for the contents, which means the summary or abbreviation of the great office celebrated in the great abbeys of the Middle Ages.

Since the first centuries, there has been in the church the cursus, i.e., series of psalms, lessons, and prayers used by monks. As centuries passed, however, these cursus became numerous books which could not be used by travelers. In 1215, Innocent III approved one of the many abridged texts that were already in use at that time, and which we call breviaries. St. Francis adopted it for his brothers who were continually on the move. This was the first breviary (according to the use of the Roman Curia). Thereafter, it was abridged, codified by the Council of Trent, and published by Pius V in 1565. Other revisions were made in the seventeenth and eighteenth centuries. A more complete reform was approved by St. Pius X in 1911. In 1945, Pius XII authorized a new version of the psalms. And in 1960, there were other modifications introduced, following the new code of rubrics.

The essential part of the breviary is made up of psalms, inspired chants taken from Holy Scripture. John XXIII has described it as " a rejoicing in truth, a daily teaching for life, consolation, and comfort in difficulties and trials." The hymns in it have a special importance. They were composed for the most part in the fourth and fifth centuries. One of the best-known authors of many of the hymns is St. Ambrose. In the thirteenth century, St. Thomas also composed hymns in honor of the Blessed Sacrament; and more recent authors have composed some for the new liturgical feasts.

The language of the breviary for the whole Western Church is Latin. It is the ardent desire of the church that the faithful also unite themselves to the priest for the recitation or the chanting of the divine office, at least for some of its parts, such as vespers.

On different occasions, John XXIII addressed profound exhortations to the clergy and religious on the dignity and beauty of the divine office, and on the spiritual wealth of its content, which is capable of satisfying the deepest needs of every priestly soul. Let us mention only the apostolic exhortation *Sacrae laudis,* of January 6, 1962, where he said among other things: " The office recited each day by priests, in spite of the differences of rite, of language, of diocese, and of religious groups is a divine poem of incomparable beauty by which the praises of God are worthily sung by the human family redeemed by Jesus Christ. . . . While turning the pages of this poem with a devout hand, strengthened by the certitude of the future glory which is in his soul, the priest finds the joy of truth, a daily lesson of life, consolation, and comfort, in difficulties and trials." And we know that in this exhortation all those who are held to the daily recitation of the divine office are invited to apply it, in union with the Holy Father, to the happy success of the Ecumenical Council.

THE LITURGICAL YEAR

The liturgical year begins with the first Sunday of Advent, i.e., the last days of November or the first days of December. It unfolds as a cycle that is like a synthesis of all human history, but it especially makes relive the principal phases of our redemption, accomplished by the incarnation, the passion, and the death and resurrection of Christ.

These cycles are centered around the feasts which recall the great mysteries of our faith: Christmas, Easter, and Pentecost.

We read in the encyclical *Mediator Dei:* " The whole year long, the celebration of the Eucharistic sacrifice and the prayers of the hours unfold themselves principally around the person of Jesus Christ. They are so harmoniously and conveniently disposed that our Lord, with the mysteries of his abasement, redemption, and triumph, occupies the first place in them."

The feasts of the saints, especially those of the Blessed Virgin, are inserted in the liturgical cycle as a witness to the fruits effected by the redemption, inviting each Christian to imitate them.

Dom Guéranger, one of the most famous initiators of the

liturgical movement of the last century, presented the liturgical year thus: " If the church renews its youth each year as the eagle (Ps. 102), it is because by means of the liturgical cycle, she is invited to do so by her Spouse, in proportion to her needs. Each year, she sees him again as a child in the manger, fasting on the mountain, offering himself on the cross, rising from the sepulcher, establishing his church, and instituting his sacraments, ascending to the right hand of his Father, and sending the Holy Spirit to men. . . . Do not practical teaching and encouragement come to us by our dear saints whose cycle is like the star? By contemplating them, we come to realize the way that leads to Christ as Christ offers us in himself the way that leads to the Father. But Mary stands out more brilliantly above all the saints, offering in herself the mirror of justice, where all the holiness possible in a pure creature is reflected."

In the last part of this morning's meeting, Cardinal Agagianian read a report on the schema prepared by his Commission concerning the sacraments and the liturgy in mission countries. The problems studied previously once again held the attention of the Central Commission, but this time only insofar as they reflected the particular conditions in which the missionaries must accomplish their task.

The church is a mother for all and she knows that her mission is to reach all souls and to offer to each one the means that are the most apt to assure its salvation.

April 2, 1962

SACRED OBJECTS

Taking up again this morning, Monday, April 2, the work of the fifth session, the Central Commission continued the examination of Chapters VI, VII, VIII, of the schema on the liturgy, already presented in part last Saturday by Cardinal Larraona. Cardinal Tisserant presided over the meeting. The chapters concerned: sacred objects, music, and art.

The church has always used for the ornamentation and splendor of cult, all the good things that nature provides and all beauty created by the human spirit. The vestments that the priest wears for the religious ceremonies, especially for the celebration of Holy Mass, the sacred vessels that are in immediate contact with the Eucharist, the very coverings of the altar, are the objects of laws that establish the material, form, and measure of their use. Everything that concerns the divine cult has its importance. The Code of Canon Law, as well as the rules of the liturgy, prescribe that each sacred object be the worthiest possible for the worship; that it be adapted to the use for which it is consecrated or blessed; and that it encourage recollection and respect on the part of the faithful.

SACRED MUSIC

Concerning sacred music, a long tradition that dates back to the beginning of Christianity exists in the church. This shows the value which she has always attributed to music because of the dignity of the divine cult and for music's effect on the soul of those who assist at sacred ceremonies.

From Gregory the Great to John XXII at the Council of Trent, the prescriptions concerning chant and sacred music reiterate that their purpose is to render homage to God and to vivify the devotion of the faithful. It is necessary, then, to avoid in them all which is profane or, worse still, sensual. In 1562 the Council of Trent, for example, prescribed: " In order that it may appear and truly be the house of the Lord, a house of prayer, it is necessary that chants and organ music which are impure and lascivious be expelled from the church."

A century later, in 1657, Alexander VII in the constitution *Piae sollicitudinis studio* recalls the rules given by preceding popes and forbids chants and music that do not become the sacred place and cult. Benedict XIV, also in 1750 in the encyclical *Annus qui,* further clarifies the ecclesiastical legislation in order that the music used in church might edify the faithful rather than scandalize them.

In recent times many important pontifical documents have been published, among others: the *motu proprio* of St. Pius X *Tra le sollecitudini* in 1903; the Constitution *Divini cultus sanctitatem* of Pius XI; the encyclical *Mediator Dei* in 1947; and the encyclical *Musicae sacrae disciplina* in 1955 of Pius XII, all of which deal with music. To these documents we must add the instruction of the Sacred Congregation of Rites in 1958 in order to complete the pontifical teachings.

SACRED ART

Side by side with sacred music, sacred art occupies, as is easily understandable, a place of prominence. It is the image and symbol of spiritual things. It can have no other end than to elevate the human soul toward heaven and to inspire it with sentiments of faith, impulses of hope, and acts of charity.

In 1903, Pius X prescribed a constitution for a commission of sacred music in each diocese. Similar dispositions concerning sacred art were also written for the dioceses of Italy by the Secretary of State in 1924. The encyclical *Mediator Dei,* in 1947, recommends the establishment of liturgical commissions. Moreover, the instruction of the Sacred Congregation of Rites of September 3, 1958, counsels, in order to obtain better results, that the three commissions (music, art, and liturgy) work not separately but together in order to counsel one another and try to solve their problems with mutual accord.

THE MISSIONS

The schema on the problem of the missions underlines, above all, the missionary commitment of the church. She has received from her founder the commission to preach the gospel to all creatures: " Go into the whole world — Jesus said to his first apostles and to the apostles of all times — proclaim the good news to every creature. He who will believe and be baptized will be saved; he who will not believe will be condemned."

This is why the problem of missions forms an integral part of the life of the church. She is " missionary " by her very nature, and she cannot renounce this characteristic, no matter what the cost may be, in order to remain faithful to the mandate which she has received: sacrifice, pouring out of blood or martyrdom. The word " mission " itself, which comes from the Latin *mittere*, i.e., " to send," is a constant reminder of the ideal of bringing all people to the truth and charity of Christ.

The missions, in the broadest sense of the word, started with the apostles and have continued through the centuries. We can cite as great missionaries: St. Augustine of Canterbury, St. Boniface, Saints Cyril and Methodius. But it is in the twelfth century, with the birth of the two great mendicant orders, the Franciscans and Dominicans, and then with the discovery of the New World, that the missions took on the proper characteristics by which they are known today.

Pope Gregory XV, in 1622, created the Sacred Congregation for the Propagation of the Faith by the bull *Inscrutabili* for the evangelization of missionary territories. Still today it directs all the countries where the hierarchy is not yet established or where the hierarchy exercises itself in vicariates and apostolic prefectures.

As we can easily imagine, the problems of the missions are, today, a little more complex, not only because of the dimensions of the world that awaits the gospel, but also because of the profound political, social, and economic evolution of many countries where missionaries work; and also because of great and ever-growing needs. We unfortunately lack the means to meet these needs.

Certain questions that were the order of the day for the Central Commission are similar to those already treated during preceding sessions on schemata developed by different Commissions. But during this session these questions were treated in the light of pontifical teaching and in particular the encyclicals: *Evangelii praecones* and *Fidei donum* of Pius XII, and *Princeps pastorum* of John XXIII. The exclusive preoccupation here was that of the needs and exigencies of the missions.

March 28, 1962

THE NATIVE CLERGY

The works of the Central Commission during this third meeting focused on the two schemata, presented by Cardinal Agagianian, on the discipline of the clergy and on religious in mission countries. These are not repetitions of the preceding schemata presented by the Commission on the Discipline of the Clergy and the Christian People. Life in mission countries, in fact, so presents situations that it is necessary to adapt common rules to very special needs.

The Central Commission this morning faced the precise problems that concern all priests entrusted with the care of souls, for example, the problem of the need for collaborators, the desirability of a common life for those who live in the same locality, the inherent difficulties of age and the lack of economic means. All these problems take on a new coloring and consequently require a new solution when they are studied from a missionary point of view.

As Pius XI said: " The apostolate is the truest and most precious substance of the Roman Pontificate." This apostolate by way of an essential requirement entails a certain number of apostles, either missionary priests or priests of the native clergy. The purpose of the former is to train the latter, i.e., their end is not only to preach the gospel but also and above all to establish new Christian communities that are capable of living independently and developing within themselves sufficient vocations to meet all the needs of religious life. The first duty of the apostles and of all missionaries has always been to prepare men who will continue their work. They choose these men as much as possible from the better candidates of the new native church founded by them. In 1944, Pius XII spoke to the directors of the pontifical missionary activities thus: " The great purpose of the missions is to establish the church in new countries and to have it become firmly rooted there, in order that it may someday live and develop without the aid of missionary endeavor. The missionary movement, then, does not have its end in itself, but rather, tends ardently toward its noble purpose and it leaves the country once it has been attained. . . . Missionary work does not limit itself to the defense and protection of its positions. Its purpose is to make a holy land of the whole world. It strives to carry the Kingdom of the risen Savior, to whom all power is given in heaven and on earth, to every continent, i.e., to establish his dominion over the hearts of all men, even to the ends of the earth."

During these past few decades, the problem of native clergy has been well met at least in certain countries, thanks to the fruitful work of missionaries during their long years of heroic sacrifices. On December 30, 1918, a few days after the end of World War I, Benedict XV strongly encouraged the formation of native clergy in his apostolic letter *Maximum illud.* This was the visible sign of the rebirth in missionary action and life after the sad years of the world conflict.

Pius XI gave a strong impetus to this missionary expansion by his encyclical *Rerum ecclesiae* of February 28, 1926. It was the same Supreme Pontiff who established institutes of missiology on a university level. These gave the theoretical and practical teaching for the formation of missionaries as well as for priests already experienced in mission apostolates. It was also Pius XI who established by Apostolic Constitution the native episcopate and consecrated six Chinese bishops in St. Peter's Basilica on October 28, 1926. Other episcopal consecrations of colored bishops followed in 1928 and 1933. Today they have become common in the life of the church.

Pius XII, in turn, from his first encyclical *Summi Pontificatus* of October 20, 1939, in which he revealed the program of his pontificate, exhorted missionaries to adapt themselves to the customs and languages of the places of their apostolate. He also reaffirmed that the church is open to the cultural, social, human, and spiritual values of every civilization.

Already in the encyclical *Evangelii praecones* of June 2, 1951, Pius XII could present a consoling report of the progress made during the twenty years following the encyclical *Rerum ecclesiae* of Pius XI: " In 1926, we counted 400 missions, now we count 600; Catholics numbered only 15,000,000 then, today they are about 20,800,000. In this same year, 1926, the priests both missionary and native numbered 14,800; today there are more than 26,800. At that time, all the chief shepherds of the missions were foreigners; in twenty years 88 of these missions were confided to the native clergy. The ecclesiastical hierarchy, furthermore, in many of these places is now set up on a regular basis with bishops chosen from the people themselves. It is also more clearly manifest that the religion of Jesus Christ is truly Catholic and that it cannot be considered a stranger in any part of the world."

These figures have increased over the past ten years, but this preoccupation remains present if we think that only eight days ago the Catholic hierarchy was established in Korea, in Vietnam in 1960, in the Belgian Congo, Ruanda-Urundi, Southern Rhodesia, and Nyasaland in 1959.

John XXIII continued in fact to press ardently for an ever-growing expansion of the missionary impetus, without losing sight of the fact that we must attain a higher percentage of native priests. In addressing the Catholic world in his missionary encyclical *Princeps pastorum* of November 28, and before recommending the collaboration of the native clergy with the missionaries, John XXIII gave new statistics illustrating the constant growth of new vocations in mission lands. He said: " We invite you to join us in thanking the Lord who has given breath to and chosen a large group of bishops and priests in mission territories; they are our dear brothers and sons opening our heart to the highest hopes. A rapid glance at the statistics for the territories under the Sacred Congregation of the Propagation of the Faith, excluding those which are now victims of persecution, show us consolingly that the first native Asiatic bishop was consecrated in 1923, and that the first native African vicars apostolic were named in 1939. Until 1959, there were 68 native Asiatic bishops and 25 native Africans. From 1918 to 1957, the native clergy increased from 919 members to 5,533 in Asia, and from 90 to 1,811 in Africa."

We can add that during 1961 alone 12 new dioceses and 2 vicariates apostolic were erected in mission lands. Moreover, 6 prefectures apostolic were elevated to the rank of diocese. There were named among the native clergy the same year: 1 archbishop and 8 residential bishops, 1 vicar apostolic, 5 auxiliary bishops, and 1 coadjutor bishop.

We all remember the moving ceremonies that took place at St. Peter's during these past few years: the presentation of the crucifix to more than five hundred missionaries before their departure, the consecration of many bishops from the most diverse areas, and the nomination of an African cardinal.

But the most significant fact that best shows Pope John's open missionary mind and heart is that in this Central Commission assembled today to discuss the schema on the clergy and religious in mission countries, there are Cardinals Tienchensin, Gracias, Tatsuo, Doi, Santos, Rugambwa, that is to say, a Chinese, an Indian, a Japanese, a Filipino, and an African. And along with these there are many missionary archbishops. There are two African archbishops, one from Vietnam and another from Indonesia.

The Council will show, therefore, by its universal plenitude and by the variety of languages, races, and colors, that the hoped-for end proposed by Benedict XV and Pius XI in the not-so-distant past have now become a consoling fact under John XXIII.

March 29, 1962

THE MISSIONARY RELIGIOUS

Today's agenda, March 29, for the Central Preconciliar Commission was again a study of the missionary problems presented by Cardinal Agagianian, president of the Commission on the Missions.

The special subject studied and discussed today, under the presidency of Cardinal Tisserant, concerned the missionaries of diverse religious orders or congregations who join the ideal of an intense apostolate among the infidels to the ideal of perfection.

The first missionaries, who converted the peoples of Europe and a few regions of Africa and Asia to the faith of Christ, did so as individuals imitating the apostles. It was more a private desire of spiritual conquest that impelled them to act than an external mandate of the ecclesiastical authority. With the advent, then, of monasticism, and especially the mendicant orders and religious congregations, special organizations were formed and adapted for a corporate missionary work that followed previously established directives and methods. The heroic, personal work of St. Francis Xavier was perhaps the last stage of a long series of similar endeavors. These were marked by famous episodes and names, but they would be unthinkable in our time.

In order to face and solve the complex problems of the missions with an efficacious organization, the missionaries today, of necessity, belong mostly to religious orders and congregations or to societies without vows, but nonetheless live a common life very close to the religious life. Their life is ordered, like the religious life, to the acquisition of perfection and the work of the apostolate.

According to the recent reports from the Congregation for the Propagation of the Faith, the ecclesiastical territories that are dependent on it number 744, of which 103 are archdioceses, 401 dioceses, 6 abbeys, 126 vicariates apostolic, 106 prefectures apostolic, and 2 missions. This last term means that the territory is not a part of a vicariate or a prefecture, but is directed by an ecclesiastical superior.

The principal religious families now dependent on the " propagation of the faith " and working in mission territories are: the White Fathers, the missionaries of Scheut, the African Missionary Society of Lyons, the Foreign Mission Society of Paris, the St. Joseph of Mill Hill Society, the African Missions of Verona, the Pontifical Institute of Foreign Missions, the Foreign Missionary Society of the United States, the St. Columban Society for Chinese Missions, the Missionary Society of the Consolata, and the Missionary Society of St. Patrick.

Many other religious families work in the missions, although they were founded for other ends. The principal ones are: the Society of Jesus, the Friars Minor, the Capuchins, the Salesians, the Benedictines, the Dominicans, the Redemptorists, the Lazarists, the Monfortans, the Verbites, and the Oblates of Mary Immaculate.

The religious missionaries today number 16,000 in Africa and Asia, where they represent 73 percent of the workers in the missions.

The majority of them come from France, Belgium, Holland, Ireland, Italy, Germany, Canada, Spain, England, Switzerland, Austria, Luxembourg, and Malta. There are also 16 other nations who have missionary sons.

The young aspirants to the missionary apostolate in the mission lands receive a special formation for the ministry in those lands after they have been formed according to the spirit of their own rule. They complete their learning in the territories to which they are assigned by becoming familiar with the language and the local customs.

Pius XII, in his encyclical *Evangelii praecones*, affirms: " It is necessary that those who are called to the missionary apostolate receive a total formation while they are still in their own country in the domain of virtue and the ecclesiastical sciences, and also acquire some familiarity with cultural and technical areas. This, then, will be of greatest use for them in their missions. They must learn foreign languages well, especially those which they will need in the countries they are assigned to. They must also be sufficiently acquainted with medicine, agriculture, ethnology, history, geography, and the other similar sciences."

One must, therefore, consider the missionary institutes or those workshops where apostolic souls are formed. These souls must always be better equipped to face the immense problems and continual evolution of the missionary world on the religious, cultural, moral, and social levels.

Pius XII, in *Fidei donum,* mapped out a synthesis of their great lines of action: " We must establish colleges and spread Christian learning in its different degrees; we must create social action organizations that animate the work of the elite Christians in the service of mankind; we must multiply all forms of the Catholic press and care for the modern techniques of communication and culture because we know the importance in our day of a well-formed and enlightened public opinion; we must above all give a greater impetus to Catholic Action and satisfy the religious and cultural needs of a generation that might seek its food outside the church, for lack of sufficient nourishment inside the church."

All this demands that the questions concerning the religious missionaries (e.g., the best means for personal sanctification, the difficulties in adjusting the religious life more closely to the pastoral life, the juridical exemption from the diocesan ordinary) examined today by the Central Commission be studied in the light of the particular conditions existing in the missions.

Religious life, which is transplanted from the original stock, be it ancient or recent, to missionary territories, can be a fruitful leaven of Christian life there, as well as a witness of evangelical perfection and an invitation to the most generous souls. Religious vocations, which have flowered during the past ten years in the mission lands, are proof of the good work accomplished and also the reward of this ever-courageous and often heroic work that the ancient orders and the new congregations have accomplished through the preaching of the gospel. They have done this by identifying themselves with the local population, by adapting themselves wherever possible to new needs, by respecting and valuing the traditions, customs, history, and civilization of each people. It is this historic fact which John XXIII underlines when he says: " Wherever the authentic values of art and thought are likely to enrich the human family the church is ready to foster this work of the mind. She, however, does not identify herself with any culture, not even Western culture, so intimately bound to her history, for her proper mission is of another order, that of the religious salvation of man. But the church, ever young with the renewed breath of the Spirit, remains disposed to reorganize, receive, and even animate everything honorable in the intellect and heart of man on other beachheads of the world than the Mediterranean basin, which was the providential cradle of Christianity."

While the Central Commission discussed the schema on religious this morning from a universal point of view, this appeal of *Fidei donum* seemed present: " Twenty more priests in this place would permit us now to plant the cross there, whereas this same land, worked by other laborers not of the Lord, will perhaps become closed to the true faith tomorrow."

Immediately after the vote on the schema concerning missionary religious, Cardinal Larraona presented a report on the third chapter of a liturgical schema; he is president of the Commission on the Liturgy.

March 31, 1962

THE CHRISTIAN LIFE AND THE MISSIONS

The first week of the Central Commission's work came to an end with the examination of three schemata on the missions, presented by Cardinal Agagianian: the discipline of the Christian people, the ecclesiastical studies, and missionary cooperation. This meeting on March 31 was presided over by Cardinal Tisserant.

The problems of the Christian life, i.e., the discipline of the faithful, are the same in substance in the countries of old Catholic tradition and in missionary countries. In fact, according to Canon Law, the laws concerning the observance of feast days, fast and abstinence, the annual confession and Paschal Communion, hold equally for all countries. The circumstances, however, that make the application of a certain law more or less easy according to the localities can vary. The principles that guide the church in her care for the spiritual welfare of all her sons remain unchanged. This concerns the enunciation of diverse precepts to favor the sanctification of all the faithful, wherever they may live. As a mother, however, the church does not wish to impose obligations that would be too heavy or difficult to realize or even contrary to the mentality and customs of the people.

This was the orientation given to the works of the members and counselors of the Central Commission. They did not lose sight of the real situation and needs of Christians in the countries of the missions.

THE LAY APOSTOLATE

Faced with the many grave dangers that menace the faith and the very foundations of Christian life, and before the terrible contest waged in different places against the church and her essential liberties, it is not sufficient to be merely a Christian — we must today become apostles. From this flows the necessity of always forming a better laity, in order that they might not only live and develop in secret the faith received at Baptism but that they might witness their faith by their example and word. St. John Chrysostom wrote: " There would be no pagans if we were truly Christians."

Pius XII in the encyclical *Evangelii praecones* encouraged the formation and organization of the laity, especially through Catholic Action: " It is absolutely necessary that the laity, uniting themselves in great number in the ranks of Catholic Action, also unite their generous and zealous activity to the hierarchical apostolate of the clergy. . . . We, therefore, desire that wherever it is possible, Catholic associations of men and women be established. Let it be thus also for the young students, workers, artisans, and athletes. Let there likewise be societies and religious associations as auxiliary troops for the missionaries. In the constitution and formation of these groups, let the qualities of the honesty, virtue, and zeal of the members be the measure, rather than their numbers."

In this matter as well as in the precepts of the church, it is not a question of copying the existing structures of organizations of other countries, but rather, of adapting methods, organizations, and proved initiatives to the exigencies of mission lands.

In the encyclical *Princeps pastorum,* John XXIII clearly indicates this way of procedure: " We will never insist enough on the necessity of adapting this form of the apostolate (Catholic Action) to the local conditions and exigencies. It is not sufficient to transfer elsewhere what has been successful in one country; but directed by the hierarchy and in a spirit of joyful obedience to the sacred pastors, the organization of this apostolate must not be overburdened and allow precious energies to be wasted by excessively specialized fragmentary movements. These could be necessary elsewhere, but would be less useful in a completely different set of circumstances and needs."

What is important in the lay apostolate either in the missionary countries or elsewhere is a deep spiritual formation, a respect for the hierarchy, and a union of those who work for the sole ideal of the triumph of Christ.

THE SEMINARIES OF THE MISSIONS

Here again the fundamental problems are the same as elsewhere, but the special difficulties in mission lands are the lack of means and personnel. The first preoccupation of bishops and missionaries is the erection of new seminaries, the quest for vocations, the spiritual and cultured formation of seminarians and clerics, the prudent selection of candidates for the priesthood, and the early pastoral training of young priests. Canon Law fixes for all dioceses the general principles regulating the life of seminaries and the organization of their studies; but there are in mission countries special needs that require and at times impose special solutions.

The actual situation of seminaries in the ecclesiastical territories dependent on the Sacred Congregation for the Propagation of the Faith is the following: in Africa there are 151 minor seminaries with 15,586 students, and 35 major seminaries with 1,875 students. In 1961, there were 111 new diocesan priests. The native clergy is continually increasing.

In India: 38 minor seminaries with 1,429 students; 10 major seminaries with 1,039 students. There were 111 new diocesan priests in 1961, the same number as in Africa. The native clergy is a little more than 3,000 priests, i.e., 72 percent of the total.

In Pakistan: 1 major seminary at Karachi with 24 students. There are 74 native priests.

In Burma: 4 minor seminaries with 227 students and 1 major seminary with 36 students. There are 94 Asiatic priests.

In Ceylon: 6 minor seminaries with 398 students, 1 regional seminary with 145 students. There are 356 Asiatic priests. Four of the 6 dioceses are governed by native priests.

In Indonesia: 16 minor seminaries with 1,548 students; 6 major seminaries with 153 students; and about 1,350 Asiatic priests.

In Indonesia: 16 minor seminaries with 40 students and 94 native priests.

In Korea: 2 minor seminaries with 307 students and 1 major seminary with 286 students. There are more than 200 native priests.

In Hong Kong: 1 minor seminary with 38 students and 1 major seminary with 11 students.

In Formosa: 3 minor seminaries with 78 students.

In Japan: 2 major seminaries with 256 students and 385 native priests.

There are countries where because of war or Communist invasion, Catholic life and seminaries are experiencing a painful setback: in China, North Korea, North Vietnam.

THE MISSIONARY SOCIETIES

The pontifical missionary societies (namely, the Propagation of the Faith, St. Peter the Apostle, the Holy Childhood, and the Missionary Union of the Clergy, which for years have labored with fruit to make the missionary problems known to the faithful of all categories and ages, in order that they might provide the efficacious help of their prayers and offerings) have need themselves of being better known. They must also work for a greater cohesion and reciprocal collaboration.

The Pontifical Society for the Propagation of the Faith was born in France in 1820, thanks to the initiative of Pauline Jaricot. The centenary of her death is this year. Her purpose was to help the missions by prayers and gifts. Since 1922, the central office has been in Rome. It is organized in such a way as to keep in touch with the most scattered parishes by means of parochial commissions dependent on diocesan committees. These committees depend on national counselors who are themselves dependent on the superior general council in Rome. In 1960 this society collected more than a million dollars which, however, satisfied no more than 30 percent of the demands made. Since 1926 this society has organized World Missionary Day.

The Pontifical Society of St. Peter the Apostle was also born in France in 1889. It was an answer to a demand for aid by a missionary bishop from Japan desirous of forming a native clergy in that country. It spread and developed rapidly with the encouragement of Leo XIII and was enriched with indulgences. In 1920, it became dependent on the Sacred Congregation for the Propagation of the Faith and its central office was transferred to Rome in 1929. Its purpose is to help existing seminaries and to found new ones for the formation of native clergy by means of annual collections. It has also established scholarships for students. The College of St. Peter the Apostle in Rome is dependent on this society. There are 102 students from 25 nations of the 5 continents actually studying here: 59 from Asia, 27 from Africa, 12 from Oceania, 2 from Europe, and 2 from America.

The Pontifical Society of the Holy Childhood was founded in France in 1843 by the bishop of Nancy, Monsignor de Forbin-Janson. Its purpose was to develop among children a love for the missions and to collect offerings from them for youth activities in mission lands. Children up to the age of twelve can take part in this work. Its headquarters are in Paris. Last year the offerings exceeded six million dollars. This is a considerable figure, but not adequate to the needs.

The Pontifical Missionary Union of the Clergy was founded in Italy in 1916 by Father Paolo Manna, who belonged to the Pontifical Institute of Foreign Missions. Its purpose was to have priests who lived and worked outside missionary lands also participate in missionary endeavors. Benedict XV, in 1918, strongly recommended it to the clergy of the entire world. Its secretariat was established in Rome in 1936. In 1956, Pius XII bestowed the title of " pontifical " on it. Today this work has about 250,000 members not counting those behind the Iron Curtain (about 30,000). These latter can no longer give news of their activity. There are 52 national central offices throughout 5 continents.

All these deserving societies foster love for the missions and collect material assistance. They also inculcate in everyone, children and the upper classes, priests and laity, the duty of prayer by making the invitation of Christ always actual: "Pray that the Lord may send workers into the harvest."

April 2, 1962

PRESS AND ENTERTAINMENT

During the second part of this morning's session, April 2, the Central Commission heard the report of Monsignor O'Connor, archbishop of Laodicea in Syria, and president of the Pontifical Commission for Cinema, Radio, and Television.

It is accepted procedure to hail the instruments of social communication as widely used means today for diffusing thought and news, for developing culture, and for fostering a better use of leisure. These means are the press, radio, the cinema, and television. Even if the press is different under certain aspects from these other technical means often called audio-visual, it has, however, many points in common with them, especially in its power to inform and influence the formation of public opinion. It is precisely under this common aspect that these means were studied, first by the Secretariat for the Press and Entertainment and then today by the Central Commission. Their purpose was to obtain from these means an ever greater service for the whole of human society. Society needs to be informed about daily events and at the same time to be elevated to a real knowledge of the spiritual world, which must find grounds for instruction and education even in entertainment.

It is the first time that these subjects studied today by the Central Commission have ever been previewed by a Council. The Code of Canon Law itself, which mentions newspapers only once, does not even allude to radio, the cinema, and television, because these are too recent. But now these have entered the homes and lives of millions of people and can no longer be ignored or underestimated.

Let us cite a few statistics: there are over 8,000 dailies in the world, selling a total of 290,000,000 copies; 22,000 diverse periodicals with a total of 200,000,000 copies.

There are 170,000 theaters with an annual attendance of 18,000,000,000 spectators.

We count 6,000 radio stations and 400,000,000 receivers; about 1,000 television stations with about 120,000,000 receivers. And it was recently announced that it will be possible to transmit television programs from one continent to another by artificial satellites.

These instruments, collectively or separately, have an incalculable power of penetration and persuasion. As news and pictures are transmitted, so are opinions, doctrines, and principles also diffused. These rapidly modify the habits and mores, as well as ways of thinking and living. These, then, directly touch the minds and consciences of men. Does the church, therefore, have the right to intervene, if only to safeguard the fundamental rights of man with his Christian dignity and immutable principles of truth and goodness, in the case of attempts to corrupt or to propagate error?

Here are some recent pontifical documents, especially on the cinema: the encyclicals *Vigilanti cura* of Pius XI and *Miranda prorsus* of Pius XII; also the discourses of John XXIII to journalists. These clearly show the religious and moral motives that guide the church in her pronouncements, at times to condemn, at times to encourage, but always to guide to the greater good of individuals and society.

THE CHURCH AND LIBERTY IN THE PRESS
AND ENTERTAINMENT

Concerning the many problems discussed today — the freedom of information, the liberty of art, and the liberty of describing evil — the church has a sure doctrine. This doctrine is inspired by Holy Scripture, the texts of the fathers and doctors of the church, and by the teachings of the Supreme Pontiffs. It is not in the spirit of the church, as it has been at times affirmed, to oppose what is new or even materially beneficial for man. The church rejects no invention or human conquest, but she intends to use all the discoveries of the mind and science to give glory to God, to educate the hearts and conscience of men, to popularize what is good, and to secure peace for all peoples. Although she condemns in the press and theaters what offends God, mutilates or deforms truth, weakens moral principles, promotes corruption, teaches or counsels evil and spreads hatred, she does not impede liberty but tries only to restrain license, whatever its form might be.

The church knows, moreover, that her mission, which she could never renounce, is to recall to each category of persons their particular duties toward the diverse media of social communication. There are those who work in and with these media: journalists, directors, producers, actors, etc. They cannot dispense themselves from the moral law that regulates all human action. There are others who use these media: lecturers, auditors, and spectators. For these also, there are laws that cannot be violated without grave moral danger. Certain others have the duty of being vigilant and of guiding the use of these media: these are parents, masters, educators, and priests. Finally, civil authority itself has the duty to defend and protect the good morals and common good of its citizens, while respecting their liberty.

The Central Commission studied these vital and important problems with serenity and depth. It was perfectly conscious that it must indicate to men and to the society of our times the indispensable values of the spirit and conscience as the supreme ideal for the media of modern social communication.

April 3, 1962

THE TEACHING ACTION OF THE CHURCH

The Holy Father opened this morning, April 3, 1962, the last meeting of the fifth session of the Central Commission, and he addressed the assembly of members and counselors present.

The Holy Father entered the Hall of the Congregations accompanied by the major-domo, Monsignor Callori di Vignale, and the secretary-general of the Central Commission, His Excellency, Monsignor Felici. After the recitation of the *Adsumus,* the prayer composed by St. Isidore of Seville which usually opens these preparatory meetings, the Holy Father sat at the presiding table, expressing his satisfaction for the work accomplished and encouraging those present to continue to pursue zealously the work still to be done until the very end.

After giving his apostolic blessing and wishing all a Happy Easter, the Holy Father left the hall. The Commission immediately examined the constitution schema on the media of social communications, i.e., the press, television, radio, and the cinema. The different parts of the schema were presented by Archbishop O'Connor, president of the Secretariat for the Press and Entertainment.

In modern society, there is hardly anyone who is not influenced more or less, often in an unconscious manner, by the lectures and performances which they attend. Youth especially are the most easily taken in due to their lack of knowledge, their curiosity, or imprudence.

What Pius XII said in 1957 about the cinema, radio, and television in the encyclical *Miranda prorsus* can also be applied to the press with some modifications: " These technical media which, we can say, are now available to all, exercise an extraordinary power on man. They lead him to the kingdom of light, nobility, and beauty as well as to the domain of darkness and deprivation. He is open to the influence of the nature of the scenes proposed to his senses."

Faced with sad fact often reported in the press, the church has always striven to follow true principles in her teachings: the spiritual and moral formation of each Christian, which enables him to judge and choose, to elicit initiative, to exercise a positive influence on the attitudes, productions, and programs of the different media of social communications. This action is carried out by the spiritual and technical formation of its personnel. In December of 1960, Pope John XXIII told Catholic journalists that a purely negative attitude of condemnation was useless, and he emphasized, on the other hand, the positive work that an exemplary Catholic can do by making these media of social communications more wholesome: " It would be in vain to abandon these to lamentations and recriminations. We must build, dear sons, and we must lead by laying the foundations of a new, a more wholesome, just, and generous era. We must aspire ardently to immediate success; we must sow, even though at times our heart is oppressed by a profound sadness, confident of seeing realized the promise of a joyful harvest. . . . We improvise no task; and if every profession with a social responsibility requires long and hard years of theoretical and practical preparation, then certainly this is also true for militant journalists. Journalists are not easily formed. To acquire that combination of gifts which make the service of the journalist easy and profitable, an apprenticeship is necessary. He must have the delicacy of the doctor, the perspicacity of the lawyer, the versatility of the man of letters, and the sense of responsibility of the educator."

What is said of journalists is also, in substance at least, applicable to producers, actors, singers, authors of comedy and television drama, and to others also. The conditions in which the church finds herself differ from country to country. This is why we would not suggest a unique formula to solve the serious problems of the moral and religious order which each medium of social communication presents. Initiative, therefore, could be different according to need and place. Catholics everywhere, however, conscious of their dignity and responsibilities must feel themselves engaged with the hierarchy, either to prevent a catastrophe through the abuse of an erroneously understood liberty or to use the media at their disposal for the profit of apostolic work, and finally to support by their voluntary offering the life and development of these media. In many countries special days are celebrated for the double purpose of keeping awake the vigilance of the faithful and of recalling the duty of cooperation with their countries.

THE NATIONAL OFFICES OF THE CINEMA

Pius XI had already prescribed that a permanent national office be established in every country. This office would encourage good films and establish a moral standard that would be publicized for both the clergy and faithful. Pius XII, in turn, recalled the need of these national and international offices not only for the cinema but also for radio and television: "After a mature consideration of the apostolic opportunities that these techniques offer, and of the need to protect the morale of Christian people which is often menaced by harmful performances, we desire that these offices be established without delay in every country where they do not already exist, and that they be entrusted to competent persons under the direction of a priest chosen by the bishop. Because the many problems that must be faced cannot always find an adequate solution in each country, it will be very useful for the national offices to work in unity with the great international organization approved by the Holy See.

THE PONTIFICAL COMMISSION FOR
CINEMA, RADIO, AND TELEVISION

It was Pope Pius XII also who instituted in 1948 " a pontifical commission for didactic and religious cinema," which became in 1952 " the Pontifical Commission for the Cinema." Its task is to study attentively diverse questions concerning the cinema, radio, and television that have some bearing on the problem of faith and morals. Finally, John XXIII, again broadening the scope of the Commission, decided that " it would have a permanent and stable character as an office of the Holy See for the examination, support, and direction of the diverse activities in the area of cinema, radio, and television."

The president of this Pontifical Commission since its foundation has been His Excellency, Bishop O'Connor; he is also the president of the pontifical Secretariat for the Press and Entertainment.

ASPECTS PROPER TO EACH MEDIUM
OF SOCIAL COMMUNICATION

The different media of social communication — press, cinema, radio, and television — were examined by the Central Commission not only under their common aspects but also under their specific characteristics. The Central Commission, then, studied their importance, power, and their influence on individuals in society.

Each one of these media has its scope of action, efficacy, and positive and negative aspects: the press with its different categories, its multiplicity of content, its exigencies of liberty in order that it might inform itself and others; the cinema, with its great possibilities of diffusion and attractive power; radio and television, with their ability to penetrate into each home and to unite people. The church has already given wise directives for each one of these media. Her directives are always valid even after many years because they flow from immutable principles and are totally free from any self-interest or partisan influence.

The pontifical teachings on the press are contained in the many discourses of Pius XII and John XXIII. We also find explicit admonitions in the documents of Pius IX, Leo XIII, Pius X, Pius XI, and especially John XXIII. Pope John has often shown a special benevolence to journalists and has given fundamental directives to the Catholic press in particular. But there has not yet been an encyclical totally dedicated to this problem until now.

The first interest shown in the cinema by the Sacred Congregation of the Consistory dates back to 1912. There have already been two encyclicals on this matter: *Vigilanti cura* in 1936, and *Miranda prorsus* in 1957. There were two discourses in 1955 by Pope Pius XII on the ideal film plus the later *motu proprio Boni Pastoris* of John XXIII. The encyclical *Miranda prorsus* also deals at length and in depth with the questions of radio and television. These two have also been the subject of many discourses by Pius XII and John XXIII.

The other media of social communication, e.g., the book and the theater, or of less importance, the tracts, manifestos, or other media of the same kind, illustrations and records, were not extensively examined by the Secretariat because the general principles regarding press, cinema, radio, and television can be applied to them.

The Central Commission, in closing the works of the fifth session with a panoramic view of the great problems of information and of the formation of public opinion, showed that it was in touch with the problems and needs of our time. It showed that it had a realistic and serene vision of the good and evil which surround us, and that it was interested solely in using what man has created in the development of technical progress and culture for the service of souls and Christian civilization.

SIXTH SESSION

May 3, 1962

THE BISHOPS

Today, May 3, at nine thirty A.M., the Central Preparatory Commission of the Second Ecumenical Council of the Vatican opened its sixth session. At the beginning of the session, the cardinal dean, Eugene Tisserant, announced to those present that the Holy Father had celebrated the votive Mass *De Domino nostro Jesu Christo, summo et aeterno sacerdote* for each of the fathers. The members and counselors received this announcement with great gratitude. Once again it showed the paternal care of the Holy Father and his solicitude for the works of the Council.

Then, Paolo Cardinal Marella, president of the Commission for Bishops and Diocesan Government, presented two schemata of decree: the first on the coadjutor and auxiliary bishops, the second on the mission of the bishop in the ministry of souls. These subjects are of vital interest and always of great pertinence because it is the activity and holiness of the bishops that gives impetus and vigor to the spiritual and moral life of a diocese. According to the expression of St. John the Evangelist, they are by their magisterial and pastoral ministry " the witnesses of light," which is Christ.

THE COADJUTOR AND AUXILIARY BISHOPS

The bishop, as the successor of the apostles, is chosen to direct and govern, in close union with the Supreme Pontiff, a part of the church. All his activity, then, is inspired by this supreme law: to save the souls that are confided to his care, as sheep to a shepherd and for whom he must give an account to God. This shows immediately how the mission of the bishop is at the same time important and serious. St. Augustine already affirmed that the difficulties, obligations, and responsibilities of bishops are unparalleled. Each period of history has had its own problems which demanded and received solutions. It is not an exaggeration to say that from the century of St. Augustine to our own days, in spite of the new means that permit a more efficacious apostolate for the conquest and salvation of souls, we have seen obstacles increase in number and importance, obstacles brought up to frustrate the spiritual instruction and formation — in a word, the sanctification of the faithful.

At times, the inherent difficulties of the pastoral ministry of our time and circumstances are apt to render the normal development of this action even more difficult. The precarious condition of a man's health, e.g., his old age or again the excessive size of the diocese of which he is pastor. In such circumstances, the church usually gives a helper to the bishop, either a coadjutor or an auxiliary.

According to the actual norms of the Code of Canon Law, a coadjutor is given to the bishop, with or without the right of succession. When the coadjutor is given to the bishop without the right of succession, he is called an auxiliary.

The rights and duties of a coadjutor and auxiliary bishop for the Latin Church are specified in canons 350–355 of the present Code.

Since the first days of the church it was customary to designate a coadjutor in case of need. St. Gregory Nazianzus and St. Augustine of Hippo, for example, were coadjutors before occupying their respective sees as venerable ordinaries. The Council of Trent, by abrogating in a general way the rights of succession to ecclesiastical benefices, made a formal exception for coadjutor bishops in case " of urgent necessity," or for the " evident utility " of a diocese.

THE PASTORAL MISSION OF THE BISHOP

By undertaking these problems which certainly are of great importance for the fervor and pastoral life of a diocese, the Central Commission shows that it is sensitive to the exigencies of its time. It also shows that, more than ever before, the ever-vigilant and effective presence of the pastor in the midst of his flock, menaced on all sides by dangers, is required.

The bishop, in fact, must be the master and doctor of the faith, father and pontiff, the shepherd at the service of his flock, and the spouse of the church. All these different aspects were studied and discussed today from a doctrinal and practical point of view and in the light of pastoral experiences, especially those of the past few decades. The Commission considered the spiritual needs of men and the negative and positive aspects that characterized on a religious plane our historical era which is socially disturbed and overflowing with deep desires of renewal but also dominated by desires that are often limited to material well-being and enjoyment alone.

THE CO-WORKERS OF THE BISHOP

In order to accomplish their tasks, which are becoming heavier, the bishops feel an urgent need today of obtaining co-workers, either by cultivating ecclesiastical and religious vocations or by using all the energies of priests and religious men and women which are at times neglected. They also prepare laymen who are not only determined to live their faith as individuals but are also capable of exercising an active and efficacious apostolate by the word, writing, art, and all the media that modern technology puts at their disposal in the domain of culture, information, and leisure.

They also, finally, establish and strengthen social and charitable organizations, works, and associations. These latter are the living expressions of the church's presence in modern society. The church has always been an incomparable mother and teacher, and she is always near to each and every one of her sons in sharing intimately their aspirations and hopes.

THE EPISCOPAL COLLEGE

If the problems of each diocese are many and weighty, the problems of the whole church are innumerable and enormous. The bishop can no longer live isolated in his see, caring only for his flock, be it large or small, but he shares the anxieties of all the church's needs. By national episcopal conferences he becomes aware of the situation in his own country, and he comes face-to-face with the methods of the apostolate. He can obtain and offer men and money to attain a common or particularly urgent objective.

Also, by means of continual contacts with the Holy See, he can truly make all the church's preoccupations his own. He can assist to the measure of his ability in the solution of the more urgent problems that confront the missionary countries, or those lacking clerics, or again those which are confronted with certain material or moral calamities. The bishop is united to the pope, and although subject to him, he experiences in him, as St. Paul says, " the solicitude of the whole church."

It is then in the spirit of fraternity and cooperation that the church can truly call herself Catholic.

The two schemata presented this morning are of fundamental importance. There is, then, a leaven that is a reason for hope and at the same time, as Pope John often says, " a pledge of renewal and updating for the whole exterior life of the church."

May 4, 1962

THE PASTORAL CARE OF IMMIGRANTS
AND REFUGEES

Continuing yesterday's discussion based on a report concerning the pastoral ministry of bishops, presented by Paolo Cardinal Marella, president of the Commission for Bishops and Diocesan Government, the members and counselors of the Central Commission examined today, May 4, the new means and methods that have become necessary in the apostolate. These have become necessary because of the special situation in which certain categories of the faithful (immigrants, seamen, aviators, nomads, and tourists) find themselves, or to bring back all "who are far away" to the faith and practice of Christian life.

Modern times, with its multiple technical inventions, imposes on the shepherds of dioceses, and through them on their collaborators, a pastoral ministry whose methods are always better adapted and whose means are always more copious. A quiet apostolate, if ever there was such, which consists above all in keeping a flock well circumscribed, is now something of the past. People today move from one region, nation, or continent to another for motives of travel, commerce, sports, and tourism. This is the phenomenon of emigration under all its forms: internal, within the same country, or external, from country to country; definitive, with a total rerooting, or temporary, with a more or less frequent or prolonged absence from one's native land.

Beyond emigration properly so called, there are the refugees, a phenomenon of all times, but one that has become more serious in these latter years. There are families dispersed by war. Individuals and large groups are uprooted by social and political maladjustments, and these afterward seek the means of rebuilding their lives outside their native land. The recent " refugee year " brought to the attention of the whole world the situation that often becomes dramatic when all human values, and especially the spiritual and religious values, become imperiled and are even trampled underfoot.

There has never been a lack of generous initiative in aiding abandoned persecuted brothers. These individual and collective efforts show in a concrete way the living presence and efficacy of the church in the midst of human suffering. The daily charitable and social works show that the words of St. Paul, *Caritas urget nos,* have in no way lost their strength. Many works witness the presence of the church today and always, although the greatest and most beautiful part of what has been accomplished in the name of and for the love of Christ can only be written in the book of God.

In the Apostolic Constitution *Exsul familia,* the tenth anniversary of which will be celebrated next August and which remains the Magna Carta of the apostolate among immigrants, it is said that " our holy mother the church, urged by her great love for souls and desirous of fulfilling the duties flowing from the mandate to save all humanity, which has been confided to her by Christ, has not delayed in taking up the spiritual care of pilgrims, strangers, exiles, and of all emigrants, without sparing her strength, and relying primarily on priests. These priests, by the administration of sacramental graces and the preaching of the divine word, have zealously labored to confirm the Christians in the faith by strengthening the bonds of charity."

This passage allows us to understand how vast and difficult is the pastoral ministry incumbent, especially in our day, on many bishops. As Pius XII said in 1952, commenting in the Constitution *Exsul familia:* " Experience teaches that once a man is uprooted from his land and moves to a strange soil, he loses a good part of his personal security and we would almost say of his human dignity." This transplantation strikes at and weakens, at least on an affective level, his most intimate spiritual sentiments and even his religious life itself. Time and persevering effort is needed to assist man to establish himself and, so to speak, root his Catholic faith in these new and different conditions in order to help him to live a normal life. This intermediary stage becomes for many the occasion of dangerous crises. We see not only that the story of the prodigal son is repeated in the most varied forms but also that the lost sheep no longer know their way. These people, then, have a greater need of the support, aid, counsel, advice, and spiritual assistance of a priest.

The rules for the pastoral ministry of emigrants are contained in the six chapters of the second part of the Constitution *Exsul familia*. The first part recalls what the church has done through the centuries for all those who were uprooted in one way or another from their native country, and transplanted in a foreign land. This first part particularly underlines the work of these recent popes: Leo XIII, St. Pius X, Benedict XV, and Pius XI.

The second part is concerned with the jurisdiction of the Sacred Congregation of the Consistory concerning emigrants. It also deals with the ecclesiastical delegate for emigration, the mission of directors, the missionaries and chaplains for emigrants, and finally the spiritual care that the bishop must have for emigrants. There is a wealth of practical directives in this document such as we have never seen before.

The problems of the chaplaincy of emigrants are cared for today by the Supreme Council of Emigration established by Pius XII on August 1, 1952, in the heart of the Sacred Congregation of the Consistory. St. Pius X had already established, in 1914, a section in this congregation " for the spiritual care of emigrants of the Latin rite." The international general secretariat for the apostolate of the high seas, recognized by Pius XI in 1922, was also established in 1952. Its high direction was confided to the Sacred Congregation of the Consistory by Pius XII. The president of the Council, as well as the secretariat, is Bishop Francesco Carpino, the assessor of the Sacred Congregation of the Consistory.

SEAMEN, AVIATORS, NOMADS, TOURISTS

We can consider seamen equally with emigrants because of their particular manner of life. Seamen spend long periods of time on ships and can rarely see their own pastor.

Those whose work is air transportation, from pilots to hostesses, need special forms of religious assistance because their work obliges them to live in a quasi-habitual manner away from home and often in non-Catholic countries.

This is why, in 1958, Pius XII commissioned the Sacred Congregation of the Consistory to study the possibility of establishing an "apostolate of the sky," modeled on "the apostolate of the sea," to care for the spiritual needs of airline crews.

Under other aspects, the professional nomads (Hungarian and Spanish Gypsies), who move around in cycles from country to country, have special religious needs on a spiritual plane. There are also the ever-growing and frequent groups of tourists who represent a sort of emigration.

"THOSE WHO ARE FAR"

The church is the mother of all men and wants to save them all whatever their profession may be or whatever country they inhabit. This is why the Central Commission, in relation with the pastoral ministry of bishops, examined this morning the innumerable problems of a spiritual and moral order inherent in these ancient and new forms of life. Once again she is the mother who follows her sons on every road of the world to lead them to salvation.

Even those who have in some way betrayed her, "those who are far," are her sons. Because they are particularly unhappy sons, she strives with a special predilection to find new apostolic methods to help them and a new language to dissipate the errors that becloud their intellects, and to bring the message of salvation to them, since they also have been redeemed by the blood of Christ.

The church must bear witness to the truth in the different situations that present themselves. Her bishops, as masters, shepherds, and pontiffs in total communion with the successor of Peter, and in full submission to his authority, are the perpetuators of the work of redemption in the territories entrusted to their pastoral solicitude. When we block their work, or prevent it, as is the case today in the church of silence, they continue to be for the faithful as well as their persecutors true fathers and sanctifiers of their souls by their prayer and at times by their blood.

May 5, 1962

RELIGIOUS INSTRUCTION

The work of the Central Commission was pursued this morning, under the presidency of Eugene Cardinal Tisserant, with the examination of certain schemata of decree, presented by Pietro Cardinal Ciriaci, president of the Commission on the Discipline of the Clergy and the Christian People. These concerned the religious instruction to be given to children and adults, to practicing Christians as well as to those who manifest hostility or indifference toward the church.

From the pastoral ministry of bishops to the one of pastors, considered especially in their functions as masters of the truth by the teaching of catechism, the most important task of the church is to teach the good news according to the mandate received from Christ: " Go into the whole world, proclaim the good news to every creature. He who will believe and be baptized will be saved; he who will not believe will be damned."

This task is accomplished by the church mainly in her catechetical teaching given first of all to children, then to adults, according to the capacity of both. The Supreme Pontiffs have often insisted on the duty incumbent on pastors to make known as deeply as possible to their faithful the truths to be believed, the virtues to be practiced, and the means of sanctification to be employed. The schema examined today by the Central Commission, based on the experience of the past, and making the needs of the present evident, traced the guidelines to be followed in order to arrive at truly efficacious catechetical teaching. At the same time it also underlined three very important aspects that mutually complement themselves: catechism manuals, the organization of catechetical teaching, and the method to be used.

THE CATECHISM

The word " catechism," of Greek origin, indicates either a book that contains a summary of the truths of faith and Christian morals, or the content itself of the book, that is to say, the brief, precise, simple exposition of the doctrine in a question-and-answer form. In this second meaning, the word " catechism " may signify " Christian doctrine."

Many have been the catechisms, always identical in the substance of their teaching, that vary in the mode of presenting truths, according to the needs of the times and the education of the readers. The best known, before the Council of Trent; was the one composed by St. Peter Canisius in three editions: the great catechism, more widespread among catechists and educated people; the succinct minor catechism for persons of average culture and students; and the little catechism, very simple and reduced to fifty-nine short chapters, for children and uncultured people.

Some attempts at unifying the catechisms were made in Italy, at least as partial experiments, from 1765 on. In 1905, in the encyclical *Acerbo nimis* (a fundamental document regarding the catechism), St. Pius X wanted " a unique text, at least for all Italy, corresponding to the desires of all." In 1913, he published the catechism that still bears his name. In Austria, a unique catechism was distributed in 1894; in Germany in 1924; in France in 1928; and in Holland in 1948.

The matter of the unique catechism has its importance, and there are good reasons which support its use, at least in a relative form, that is to say, on a national plane, especially if we keep in mind the facility with which the faithful today move from one place to another and change residence. The truths certainly are always the same, but at times the way of expressing them could evoke astonishment, if not scandal, especially for more simple souls. On the other hand, we must also keep in mind the diversities of people with regard to mentality, spiritual preparation, and culture.

CATECHETICAL ORGANIZATION

Organization is, we might say, the characteristic of our age. We must not be astonished, therefore, if the church herself makes use of it to accomplish better her task of instructing the faithful in the faith.

Pius XI, in June, 1923, by the *motu proprio Orbem Catholicum*, instituted in the Sacred Congregation of the Council a catechetical office. This office was to condense and strengthen as much as possible, throughout the entire world, the teaching of Christian doctrine, essential and indispensable for those who want to know, practice, and defend the faith. In 1932, he proclaimed St. Charles Borromeo and St. Robert Bellarmine the patrons of all catechetical undertakings.

The Code of Canon Law devotes the whole first chapter of the title XX to catechetical teaching. Canon 1329 says expressly: " It is a special and very serious duty, particularly for the pastors of souls, to occupy themselves with providing instruction of the Christian people," and the following canons made more precise the obligations of pastors toward children about to receive the sacraments of Penance and the Eucharist, and toward adolescents and adults.

One of the principal reasons why individuals and whole groups of Christians abandon the church and religious practice is ignorance regarding the truths of the faith. The phenomenon of atheistic Communism, so widespread today in certain ancient Christian countries, is also, in large part, aided by the church's inability to contact large segments of the population. From this stems the church's desire to organize catechetical teaching, making use of all the modern means at her disposal, including the press, radio, and television, so it will penetrate always more deeply into society.

In order that the organization be efficacious, sensitive and active national and diocesan promotion centers are necessary. The Central Commission equally considered this question.

METHODS OF TEACHING

Catechetics is a science. It is the art of teaching, and it must use all the resources of psychology and pedagogy. In fact, the teaching of catechism cannot limit itself to the learning of formulas learned by heart. We must start with this and then proceed to the comprehension of the truth, to its assimilation, to the education of the heart and the mind, and finally to the living of the truths.

This is what Pius X wrote in 1912, in his letter *Fin dai primordi* (From the beginnings), which serves as the preface to his catechism: " In the first five elementary grades, the entire text of the catechism must be learned by heart in order that the fundamental truths of faith might be firmly impressed on the mind. However, it is of utmost importance that the student understand what he learns in a manner appropriate to his age. A double explanation is therefore necessary: first, for the words that are more obscure; and secondly, for the content of the formulas to be learned. But it is always equally good to force the students to express their answers learned by heart in their own words."

This is why, from knowledge to practice, from doctrine to life, catechetics must, in order to attain its end, become a science and even the science of life. Furthermore, the pastor who teaches catechism should make use of all means that techniques might offer. He should keep himself up to date in this matter by reading reviews and books. He should strive to give his lessons in the appropriate places, at the right times, and in a simple and clear form. In setting forth the doctrine, he should also make evident the practical precepts that flow from it in order to form instructed and consistent Christians.

By a happy coincidence, the Central Commission discussed the question of the catechism of the feast of St. Pius V, who, as we have said, published the first printed catechism according to the decrees of the Council of Trent.

After the schemata on religious instruction, Pietro Cardinal Ciriaci presented other schemata of an essentially moral and juridic nature to the Central Commission. Their concern was the ecclesiastical revision and condemnation of books, and also censures such as excommunication, suspension, and interdict. By these censures the church deprives Christians culpable of serious offense of certain spiritual benefits. This matter is regulated by Canon Law.

May 7, 1962

THE ESTEEM OF VIRGINITY AND CHASTITY

Resuming the work this morning, May 7, as usual at nine thirty, under the presidency of the cardinal dean, Eugene Tisserant, the Central Commission ended the vote on the schemata of decrees presented last Saturday by Pietro Cardinal Ciriaci.

The Commission then examined a schema of constitution presented by Alfredo Cardinal Ottaviani, president of the Theological Commission, on the esteem of virginity and chastity, on the dignity of marriage and family duties.

Simply mentioning these titles indicated the importance of this schema, which reflects the most acute and discussed moral problems of our day. The one who renounces, for a superior ideal, the establishing of a family does not thereby accomplish a mutilation of his personal and spiritual values, but by elevating himself above natural and legitimate instincts, gives himself to God out of love for him, both in body and in soul, i.e., his liberty and his right to propagate, in time and in a certain sense after his death, his name and life in the name and life of his children. He acquires, then, by prayers, the apostolate and sacrifice, a spiritual paternity that is a source of joy, supernatural graces, and personal fulfillment.

Everyone knows that the Catholic Church has always held virginity in high esteem as a symbol and expression of a total consecration to God and as a source and support of one's own generous gift of self to all the works of the apostolate. We also know that the Catholic Church has always given particular attention in her education to the virtue of chastity, which prepares happy and fruitful marriages.

Although naturally preferring virginity because it is more agreeable to God, the church has always fostered a great respect for marriage elevated by Jesus Christ to the dignity of a sacrament. By proclaiming, moreover, and defending without concession its unity, indissolubility and fruitfulness, the church has always shown that she considers conjugal life as the ordinary way of sanctification for the majority of the human race. By examining today these two themes in a single schema of constitution, the Central Commission shows that the church desires to underline once again the precious values of a perpetual virginity consecrated to God as well as the importance of marriage.

The matter in question is not only perpetual virginity but also that complete chastity which must be practiced by youth before marriage and by those who live for one motive or another outside of marriage. Speaking to doctors in 1948, Pius XII said: " The principle is inviolable. God alone is the master of life and of the integrity of man, of his members, his organs, and his potencies, especially those which associate him with creative work."

It is true that according to certain current theories it would be almost impossible for young people — especially in today's world — to practice purity. These theories are inadmissible by the church, which affirmed again in Pius XII's words: "We declare today to educators and to youth itself that the divine commandment of purity of soul and body holds without weakening for present-day youth. It also has the moral obligation and, with the help of grace, the possibility of keeping itself pure."

Modern life, without doubt, multiplies invitations to evil by such distractions as beauty contests, spectacles, billboards, songs, illustrated magazines, beaches, places of vacation, promiscuity, and certain forms of sport. This is why the church never ceases to recall to each one the principles of prudence, conscience, and responsibility, the rights and duties of liberty, and the obligation of vigilance and precaution on the part of parents, educators, and civil authorities. This is also why the church points out as dangerous and condemns as erroneous all theories that are then translated into practice concerning the cult of movie stars, naturalism, the so-called sexual education, pansexualism, and certain injurious aspects of psychoanalysis.

MARRIAGE

In reality what the church does to inculcate the love and practice of chastity in her sons, especially the youth, is the best preparation for marriage. And it is especially on this important theme that the Central Commission focused its attention today: i.e., on the origin, the nature and dignity, the properties, the characteristics and ends of marriage, on the power of the church and the place of the state in this domain. It also studied those errors which are directly harmful to marriage, e.g., divorce, or indirectly, Malthusianism, and artificial insemination.

THE RIGHT TO MARRY

The church, above all, precisely because she considers the practice of virginity out of love for God a most privileged ideal for generous souls, proclaims and supports the natural right to contract marriage. In an allocution of 1941, when totalitarian doctrines were forced upon certain European peoples, whereby marriage was made impossible either because of racial motives or because of barrenness by sterilization, Pius XII clarified the immutable position of the church: " In the first place, if we consider the right to marry, our glorious predecessors, Leo XIII and Pius XI, taught that there is no law which can deprive man of his natural and fundamental right to marry. This right, because it was immediately given to man by the Author of nature, the supreme legislator, cannot be refused to any man, unless he renounces this right of his own free will or by reason of mental or corporeal deficiencies making him incapable of contracting marriage. But in order that in certain cases a marriage might be prevented or that an already contracted marriage might be declared null, it is necessary to establish, with moral certitude, that an antecedent and perpetual incapacity exists. If this certitude exists, marriage cannot be permitted, and if it is already celebrated, it cannot be considered valid."

THE DUTIES OF MATRIMONY

It is clear, therefore, that precisely because marriage is a sacrament, it is a serious and sacred matter, and the spouses then must prepare themselves for its celebration, conscious of the rights and duties it entails. Pius XII again recalled to youth centers: " Our predecessors of happy memory, and particularly Pius XI in the encyclical *Casti connubii,* recalled the holy and indisputable laws of conjugal life, but we especially call to mind that in many cases a true heroism is demanded of Christian spouses in order to observe these laws inviolably."

These are useful truths to be recalled today when so many forms of hedonism menace the fundamental values of the family. The church has the mission of recalling to individuals and society, even if this goes against the grain, that individual and social duties exist. These cannot be omitted even if they become especially weighty and cumbersome by reason of exceptional circumstances.

May 11, 1962

THE SACRAMENT OF MATRIMONY

During the last part of yesterday's meeting and today's, the Central Commission examined schemata drawn up by the Commission on the Discipline of the Sacraments, presented by Cardinal Aloisi Masella, president of this Commission. The schemata examined today are on the impediments of marriage, mixed marriages, consent to marry, the celebration of matrimony, and matrimonial trials. These are extremely important subjects if we consider that marriage represents the official and sacred constitution of the family, the first cell of human society. Today marriage is threatened by many dangers ranging from divorce, which is admitted in the legislation of many countries, to a materialistic-hedonistic mentality that is ever more rampant and that intends to make marriage devoid of its sacred content by reducing it to unimportant and short-lived contracts. The documents of the church on the value and characteristics of the sacrament of Matrimony are innumerable and date back to the most ancient times. But a work of vigilance and education is especially necessary for the young in order to infuse into them deep religious convictions and help them to realize the individual and social responsibilities that marriage demands.

The actual discipline for the sacrament of Matrimony dates back to the Council of Trent and was codified in Canon Law. The laws of the church have as their purpose the maintaining of marriage as God instituted it, with all its essential characteristics: unity, indissolubility, and fecundity. By these laws the church strives to have all the faithful understand the importance and the price of the marriage contract elevated by Christ to the dignity of sacrament.

THE CIVIL EFFECTS OF MATRIMONY

Although the church admits only religious marriage as valid, she nonetheless recognizes the competence of the state in what concerns the civil effects of marriage. Concerning civil marriage, which is also imposed on Catholics in some countries, and concerning divorce, let us recall the words of Leo XIII in the encyclical *Arcanum* of February 10, 1880. This document is completely consecrated to marriage and the evils of divorce. He says: " It is important for everyone to know that a union between a Christian man and woman outside the sacrament is bad. This union has neither the value nor the character of a true marriage. Even though it could conform to civil law, it has no other value than any other ceremony or usage introduced by civil law. Civil law, therefore, can only order and regulate the consequences that marriage entails in the civil order and that evidently could not be produced if the cause were not true and legitimate, i.e., if the nuptial bond did not exist. These things should be well known and understood by spouses. They must know that they must submit themselves to laws in this matter. The church herself does not oppose these laws, because she wants and desires the effects of matrimony to be safeguarded to their fullest extent, and children to be protected from prejudice."

THE IMPEDIMENTS – MIXED MARRIAGES

The impediments of matrimony are " the circumstances relative to the contracted persons that by divine or ecclesiastical law render the persons unqualified to contract a licit or valid marriage." In ecclesiastical legislation the impediments that render marriage illicit but valid are called prohibitive impediments and are three in number: simple vows (of virginity or perfect chastity, not to marry, to receive sacred orders, or to enter religious life) ; mixed religion; and the legal bond resulting from adoption. This latter impediment exists only in countries where civil legislation considers it an impediment. The church alone can dispense from these impediments under certain conditions foreseen by Canon Law.

Invalidating impediments (i.e., those separating the spouses) render the marriage not only illicit but also invalid. These are: age (sixteen years old for men, fourteen for women), antecedent and perpetual impotence (not to be confused with sterility), preexisting marriage bond, disparity of cult, sacred orders, solemn religious profession, rape, crime, consanguinity, affinity, public dishonesty, spiritual and legal parenthood in countries where it is considered invalidating by civil law. Without entering into the many distinctions that each of these cases supposes, it is certain that the church can dispense from those impediments which are from positive ecclesiastical law, but not from those which are of natural or divine law.

Among the prohibitive impediments that the church can dispense under certain well-defined conditions is the one of mixed religion that exists between a Catholic and a non-Catholic Christian. The conditions for dispensation required by the church are: the promise that the non-Catholic will respect the religious convictions of the Catholic partner, and the promise by both to have all their children baptized and educated in the Catholic religion. This promise must be made in writing and a moral certitude must be had that it will be carried out.

Also, for the invalidating impediment of the disparity of cult which exists between a Catholic and an unbaptized person, i.e., a non-Christian, the church can also give a dispensation under the same conditions as the case of mixed religion.

THE CONSENT

The consent of the spouses is necessary and essential for the validity of matrimony, as Pius XI affirmed in the great encyclical on Christian marriage, *Casti connubii,* of December 31, 1930: "Every marriage, inasmuch as it constitutes a conjugal union between a determined man and woman, has no other origin than the free consent of each of the two spouses. This act of free will, by which each of the two partners gives and receives the rights proper to matrimony, is so necessary to effect a true marriage that no human power could take its place."

According to the Code of Canon Law, the marriage contracted by force or under duress of a serious, unjust, and external fear is invalid. Equally invalid is the marriage contracted with the positive intention of not wanting to marry, of excluding all conjugal rights and duties, or of rejecting an essential property of marriage.

Always according to Canon Law in what concerns the form of celebration, only those marriages are valid which are contracted before a pastor or local ordinary, or a priest delegated by them, and before two witnesses. In some extraordinary cases, as for example, in the danger of death, certain provisions are made.

MATRIMONIAL TRIALS

Concerning matrimonial trials, canons 1960–1962 determine what tribunal is competent, what its composition must be, what the rights and duties of the defender of the bond are, what concerns the witnesses and experts, what publication must be made, and what the appeals against the sentence are. We must not forget that the church's objective in matrimonial trials is the salvation of souls. John XXIII said to the members of the Rota tribunal last December: " The good of souls . . . , that is the spirit which inspires the church's tribunals, and consequently, the ecclesiastical judge, the defender of the bond, as well as the promoter of justice and the lawyer. . . . Yes, the church always has the eternal salvation of each in view even when she limits the right to accuse and when she passes a sentence of culpability. Even to the culpable partner, she never withdraws the means of escaping the peril of eternal damnation."

May 8, 1962

THE DOGMATIC CONSTITUTION
ON THE CHURCH

Continuing the subjects elaborated by the Theological Commission and presented by Alfredo Cardinal Ottaviani, the Central Commission pursued its work this morning, May 8, under the presidency of Eugene Cardinal Tisserant, with the discussion of a constitution schema on the church.

The dogmatic constitution approved in the fourth and last session of the First Vatican Council declared: "The Eternal Shepherd, master of our souls, in order to perpetuate the salvific work of our redemption, established the holy church in which all the faithful would be assembled as in the house of the living God, united by the bond of a single faith and charity."

Such is the church in her divine institution and in her mission which is perpetuated through the centuries in spite of conflicts, obstacles, and persecutions.

At the First Vatican Council, the dogmatic constitution on the church defined the primacy of Peter and his successors. It also defined the infallibility of the Supreme Pontiffs in matters of faith and morals when they speak ex cathedra. The original schema, *De ecclesia,* submitted at Vatican I, was composed of fifteen chapters of which only four were discussed and approved in the Constitution *Pastor aeternus.*

The schema examined today by the Central Commission

concerns certain points and problems among those not presented at Vatican I because of the well-known historical events that interrupted the Council.

At first sight these could appear to be themes already prepared by other Commissions and already examined by the Central Commission. Such is not the case. Each subject here is considered in the light of doctrine and dogma, whereas on the other occasions, these questions were studied from a juridical, pastoral, or disciplinary point of view.

THE CHURCH, THE MYSTICAL BODY

The nature of the church is clearly brought to light in the gospel and in the teaching of St. Paul. Jesus compares the church to a kingdom that must develop in time and be completed in eternity, to a flock cared for by only one shepherd. St. Paul speaks of the church as a house, a temple, the pillar and foundation of truth, a body whose head is Christ, and whose members are the faithful. This is a wonderful reality which is being brought to greater light today because of the profound studies synthesized in the encyclical *Mystici corporis* of Pius XII. This reality has already been explicitly affirmed in the words of Jesus: " I am the vine, you are the branches; he who abides in me and I in him bears much fruit."

THE NECESSITY OF BELONGING TO
THE CHURCH TO BE SAVED

By examining the doctrine on the nature of the church, her mission and irreplaceable function are easily understood. No one can be saved without belonging to the church, either in fact or in desire, at least implicitly. On different occasions, the Supreme Pontiffs affirmed: " You will not fail, in your teaching, to remind the flock entrusted to your care of these great and salutary truths: we cannot render God the cult which befits him and is agreeable to him; and it is not possible to be united to him, except through the mediation of Jesus Christ; and we cannot be united to Christ except in and through the church, which is his mystical body; and finally, it is not possible to belong to the church except by means of the bishops, the successors of the apostles, united with the supreme shepherd, the successor of Peter."

THE EPISCOPACY

Other chapters of the constitution schema examined today by the Central Commission concern the priesthood. The episcopacy as the supreme degree of the sacrament of Orders was studied, along with the duty and dignity of bishops who have been instituted by Jesus Christ to govern the true church together with and under the authority of the Roman Pontiff.

May 9, 1962

THE LAITY IN THE LIFE OF THE CHURCH

This morning, May 9, the discussions were continued on other chapters of the constitution schema on the church. Alfredo Cardinal Ottaviani, president of the Theological Commission, presented the material. The place and function of religious as well as the laity in the life of the church were especially studied today, thus bringing the first part of this schema (its nature, members in general, priests, and bishops) to an end.

The last chapter of the first part of this schema on the church is of special interest today because of the ever-growing importance of the laity in the life of the church. The Council is vitally interested in the eventual role that the laity will have in the many apostolic works of the modern world, " in collaboration with the hierarchical apostolate of the church," according to the definition of Catholic Action already given by Pius XI.

Over the course of the last decades, many writings have been published on the question of the laity, not only on an organizational level, but also on a specifically theological plane. We see the meaning of the word " laity " becoming more and more precise. From the first centuries of Christianity it has signified a baptized person who had received no ecclesiastical order, but who did not oppose the truths, principles, and doctrines of the church. The words " laity " and " laicism " have very different meanings. The first, religiously speaking, has a positive or at least a neutral meaning, whereas the second has a negative one.

The pontifical documents that recall the need for the lay apostolate (its orientation a guidance for a more lasting result) are becoming more frequent. Choosing them is a problem in itself. Two affirmations, however, seem particularly important. The first is an extract from the allocution of Pius XII, February 1952; the second, from the encyclical *Mater et magistra* of John XXIII. Pius XII said: " Under this aspect (the edification of the human community by means of the church) the faithful, and more especially the laity, find themselves on the front line of the church's life. Through them, the church is a vital principle of human society. . . . Each of the faithful, each man of goodwill, must examine anew, with a resolution worthy of the great movements of human history, what he personally can and must do, what contribution he must bring to the salvific work of God, to help a world that is on the road to ruin, as is the case today."

John XXIII says: " The church . . . has the right and a duty not only to defend the principles of the moral and religious order but also to intervene authoritatively in the temporal order when there is question of judging the application of the principles to concrete cases. . . . The church accomplishes this task by her sons, the laymen, who must exercise their professional activities to this end, as the accomplishment of their duty as a service that they render in intimate union with God in Christ."

The personal mission of the laity in purely human questions does not necessitate the intervention of pastoral authority, neither does it require them to be in a particular religious state. It nourishes itself, however, as does the mission of the whole church, from the same source, which is Christ, and it tends toward the same end, which is the salvation of souls.

Their mission, in the first place, has an explicit religious character insofar as it tends to build the church by prayer, example, sacrifice, word, and works, by putting these at the service of the gospel, according to the needs and methods of the modern world; by the fulfilling of their duties of an individual, domestic, and social state; and by helping the clergy in the measure of their capabilities. They thereby favor indirectly the development of religion by becoming the leaven of Christian life, where they work daily. Without leaving the state or the profession in which Providence has placed them, it is their task to sanctify, in a certain sense, the world in which they work, from within, according to the expression of Pius XII: *Consecratio mundi.* The apostolate of the laity takes on, above all, a personal form, i.e., it is an expression of faith in every trial, a spontaneous, sincere, and concrete manifestation of convictions translated into a distinctively Christian way of thinking, speaking, and acting. It is also an organized form of the apostolate in which the best energies are united to exercise a deeper influence of the Christian spirit upon all the structures (even the profane) of the modern world.

Insofar as they exercise an organized apostolate in a direct collaboration with the spiritual and pastoral work of the church, their activity must clearly be subordinated to the authority of the bishops, who, under the jurisdiction of the vicar of Christ, have been consecrated bishops by the Holy Spirit in order to feed the church of God in their respective dioceses.

" So it is that even from a social point of view this action can exercise an influence on civil society. The participation of the laity in the apostolic work of the church must be directed and guided by the hierarchy, which represents, for Catholics, the competent authority to judge the moral repercussions of the problems uncovered by the economic and social order." (Pius XII.)

But it must be said that this is only the first reference to the question of the laity, because the work prepared by the Commission for the Laity has yet to be examined by the Central Commission.

RELIGIOUS

We have always given great importance in the church to the states of perfection, i.e., the different forms of religious life, from the ancient monarchist to mendicant orders, to the religious congregations, to the societies of common life with vows, and to the recent secular institutes. Innumerable souls through the course of the twenty centuries of Christianity, by practicing the evangelical counsels of obedience, poverty, and chastity, have always given a new brightness to one of the church's notes, her sanctity. It is, in fact, from the primitive monasteries, from the convents of men as well as women, that the brightest examples of an often heroic sanctity have come. They have been nourished by the most diverse means, which range from contemplation to the spiritual and corporeal works of mercy, from penance to the apostolate in all its forms.

The Gospel parable that compares the Kingdom of God on earth, i.e., the church, to a tree, which begins as a small seed and becomes majestic and receives the birds of the sky, can also be applied to the different states of perfection. From the early time of the church, in order to answer Christ's invitation to be perfect as he and his Father are perfect, a manner of life appeared that is completely opposed to the spirit of the world. It arose in different forms, but always animated by the desire to follow Christ in his total obedience to the Father, in his poverty which owned nothing, and in his immaculate chastity.

Each new religious family can be compared to a palm that is added to the preceding branch on the trunk of the states of perfection. The rules of life, the methods of formation, the habits and the ends, vary according to the many religious families. Each one is born to answer the different and particular needs of times and places, but only one ideal animates them by conferring upon them a continuity that surpasses the motives, at times contingent, for which they were born. This ideal is to render glory to God by cooperating with the church in the salvation of souls.

OBJECTIONS AGAINST THE RELIGIOUS LIFE

We cannot consider valid the objections of those who consider membership in an order or a religious congregation as a form of diminution, not to say degradation, of the human person, as if the profession of vows prevented the free development of the individual's talents. The religious rule, as all discipline, does not intend to stifle or destroy what is good in human nature, but it strives to uproot the evil as much as possible, in order to permit the better qualities to be developed. Whoever renounces, moreover, his will, his goods, and his right to form a family does not mutilate himself, but rather, frees himself from material burdens in order better to consecrate himself to the conquest of spiritual goods.

Other aspects of the religious life set forth by Valerio Cardinal Valeri, president of the Commission for Religious, will be examined in the following days, but from a different point of view. They were examined today from a theological and doctrinal viewpoint, i.e., one that explains the spiritual and supernatural motives for which states of perfection were born and continue to prosper in the church. These produce precious fruits of good example, reparatory prayers, ecclesiastical as well as profane science, charitable works, the apostolate, and sanctity.

May 10, 1962

RELIGIOUS VOCATIONS

Valerio Cardinal Valeri presented this morning, May 10, some chapters from the schema on religious. These problems, as we have already noted, are not examined from the same point of view as when they were presented by the Theological Commission in the schema on the church. This latter schema, in fact, proposed to clarify on a doctrinal plane the position and role of religious, whereas today the discussion focused on certain practical aspects of religious vocations and the formation of young aspirants to the states of perfection.

We must here recall the terms of canon 1353: " The priests, especially the pastors, will take care that the children who show signs of an ecclesiastical vocation be carefully separated from the temptations of the world so that the seed of their vocation can be developed."

What the Code says of ecclesiastical vocations in general can be applied to religious vocations in particular. Without losing sight of the fact that because of the worldly mentality and laicism that penetrate today more and more into all milieus, religious vocations face greater difficulties in their development than do the vocations to the ecclesiastical state. The fantastic conceptions that some people have of the vows of obedience and poverty, and also the fear of penance and mortification on the part of all, converge to avert even the generous souls of youth who would think of consecrating themselves to God.

We see a necessity, consequently, to seek out, cultivate, protect, and defend vocations, be they ecclesiastical or religious, of men and of women, especially where they find a more favorable soil for birth and development. This is the case for Catholic associations. Pius XII said in the *motu proprio, Primo feliciter,* of November 12, 1948: " We paternally recommend to the directors and assistants of Catholic Action and of other associations of the faithful in whose bosom an integral Christian life is formed, to promote generously these holy vocations. The initiation to the practice of the apostolate for so many young elite who, answering a celestial vocation, aspire to a higher perfection either in religious life or in secular institutes is also found in these associations."

The desire and need for religious vocations must not, however, have us seek quantity at the expense of quality. Neither must the ideal, spirit, or constitution of a religious family be adapted in any way to increase its recruitants. The ends of each institute must be presented in their true light, and eventually in their complete vigor. We must, above all, seek the supernatural means of prayer to have God send workers into the harvest. It has always been the examples of a holy life, of a generous apostolate, and of infinite charity given by religious and the communities which are in greater contact with the world that have effectively attracted young candidates.

When an aspirant, therefore, applies for membership in an institute, a convent, or a monastery, he must find there a paternal and fraternal welcome. But his qualities and defects, his aspirations and dispositions, must, however, be the object of a prudent examination in order that no one be admitted into an order or congregation if he is not truly called there, because he could become a ravenous wolf. Superiors, spiritual directors, and even doctors have a serious responsibility each in his own domain before God and men. This could be violated either by the rejection of a true vocation after a superficial examination or by considering too rapidly as qualities what would be no more than appearances.

A vocation is no more than the beginning of a long journey. We must expect moments of lassitude and discouragement, and fortify ourselves against them inasmuch as possible. A vocation is a seed that needs care and maternal attention, once it is placed in good soil in order to grow, become strong, mature, and fructify.

THE FORMATION OF YOUNG RELIGIOUS

This is why the formation must be " sure, enlightened, solid, and truly complete," as is mentioned in the statutes annexed to the Apostolic Constitution *Sedes sapientiae,* of July 7, 1956: " Formation must be surrounded with attentive care and be carefully tested. . . . It must proceed in the light of proved scientific principles that we will apply according to the methods which have proved the most efficacious and which can still be perfected with the years."

The first formation centers on the man, his personality and natural qualities, without which the whole edifice, even spiritual, becomes as useless as a house without a foundation. All the faculties of man, at the same time, must be developed, not according to successive stages but in a harmonious and complete fashion. On a religious level, the formation must be deep, solid, and equitably based on all the truths of faith. On an ascetical level, it must prepare a man to desire mortification, the sources of spiritual consolation, and the secure way to perfection. On an intellectual level, it must give complete and open instruction according to the ways and regulations in use. On an apostolic level, it must equally fill with fervor those who have fewer natural gifts, less knowledge, and weaker health. And finally on the social level, it must give an exact knowledge of the church's doctrine as it is expressed in ancient and recent pontifical documents, in a serene and objective vision of the terrestrial realities, in order to prepare true masters and guides for the men of our times, having neither a nostalgia for the past nor an illusion of the future.

This work of forging a new man, of transforming a man full of imperfections into an apostle and saint, requires a long apprenticeship during the years of novitiate and long paternal care during the whole period of studies, and also after studies. These are exercises which engage the whole life of the religious, tending toward the securing of an always more

Christlike perfection. Humanistic and scientific studies, philosophy and theology, must all concur in an integral education of the mind and heart, of the will and conscience. Even those who do not prepare themselves for the priesthood must receive a sufficient instruction, not only to answer the aims of their community but also to be better prepared for a deeper religious formation.

May 12, 1962

THE PERPETUAL CALENDAR: A FACTOR OF UNITY WITH THE EASTERN CHURCHES

The subject discussed today, May 12, the last of the session, by the Central Commission, was on the Oriental Churches. Four schemata were presented by Amleto Cardinal Cicognani, president of the Commission for Oriental Churches. They were: the powers of the bishops, religious instruction, the perpetual calendar and the celebration of Easter, and the divine office. As we have already remarked on other occasions, these problems are almost entirely the same as those which have already been studied in a general way. But today they were studied in the light of the particular conditions of the Catholic Oriental Church.

The schema on the perpetual calendar and the date of celebrating Easter have not yet been treated. Here is a synopsis of the historical circumstances that brought it about. The calendar now in use dates back to 1582, and it is called the Gregorian calendar because Gregory XIII adopted it by the bull *Inter gravissimas,* after having the best mathematicians of the time study it. Until then we had used the Julian calendar, so called because Julius Caesar had adopted it in 45 B.C. It had many defects that were almost completely corrected by the Gregorian calendar. This latter was adopted by almost every country at different dates.

On diverse occasions, not only for religious considerations, we have attempted to remedy the imperfections of the Gregorian calendar (e.g., it has a six-day lag every ten thousand years). Universal and perpetual calendars have been prescribed with a fixed date for the feast of Easter and consequently for all the other mobile feasts (i.e., Ascension, Pentecost, and Corpus Christi). These calendars would have each year the same so that the days of the week would fall on the same days of the year.

Proposals along these lines were made by the League of Nations in 1923 and again in 1931, the United Nations in 1949 and 1950. One of the last proposals had a year composed of four trimesters of thirteen weeks each, i.e., ninety-one days. Each trimester would always begin on a Sunday and end on a Saturday. January 1 would always be a Sunday. The months would always have thirty days, except the first month of each trimester, which would have thirty-one days. The dates, thereby, would always be the same for each day of the week. The last day of the year would be considered as a double Saturday. December 30, in order not to break the equilibrium, would not be entered in the ordinary allowance, it would become a kind of " blanc " day without a date. It would likewise be for a supplementary day of the leap year. Easter, then, would always fall on Sunday, April 8.

Since the first decades of the spread of Christianity in the world, there have been different dates for the celebration of Easter in certain Oriental Churches. One custom had the celebration of Easter on the fourteenth of the month of Nisan. This is the fixed day for the Hebrew Pasch whatever might be the day of the week. Those who followed this custom were called " Quartodecimans." In the West, Easter was always celebrated on the Sunday following the full moon of spring. In the second century, the differences became more pronounced and only the prestige of saints like Polycarp, disciple of St. John the Evangelist, and Irenaeus, bishop of Lyons, permitted a relative peace.

The controversy was solved, at least formally, at the Council of Nicaea in 325, where the usage of the Western Church prevailed. The points on which the fathers of Nicaea agreed were the following: the feast of Easter would always be a Sunday; the Christian Easter would never be celebrated on the same day as the Hebrew Pasch; and Easter would always be the Sunday after the fourteenth of Nisan. According to the dispositions of the Council of Nicaea, the patriarch of Alexandria was commissioned to calculate each year the Sunday on which the celebration of Easter would take place and to announce it in due time to all the other churches.

This method was certainly not easy or definitive, for uncertainty still remained. It was only in the sixth century, thanks to the studies of Denis the Small, that a sure and scientific base was found to set the date of Easter even many years in advance. His calculations were based on the regular cycle of nineteen years.

There are also discrepancies in the date of Christmas, celebrated on December 25 by the Western Church and on January 7 by almost all the Oriental Orthodox Churches as well as by some Catholic Oriental Churches.

This brief allusion permits us to understand why the Catholic Church of the Orient is more sensitive to the problem of a universal calendar. While naturally respecting the fundamental cycle of the seven-day week, they have a desire to find a common point, if possible, with the separated brothers for the celebration of the most important Christian feasts together. This could also be a step toward a better understanding of one another.

It was on the examination of these questions concerning the Oriental Church that the Central Commission ended the works of its sixth session.

SEVENTH SESSION

June 12, 1962

SEMINARIES

Under the presidency of the cardinal dean, Eugene Tis-serant, the seventh and last session of the Central Preconciliar Commission opened this morning, June 12. After a report by Cardinal Pizzardo, the president of the Commission on Studies and Seminaries, on the general organization of studies, the spiritual formation, and the disciplinary and pastoral teaching in seminaries, a discussion began that made evident today's more vital aspects and most urgent problems of spiritual, moral, intellectual, and pastoral preparation for the candidates to the priesthood.

The seminary, as an institution, virtually unchanged in its essential lines, dates back to the Council of Trent. In the twenty-third session, canon 18, this Council decided that all the episcopal sees must "assemble a certain number of students, give them religious instruction, and form them to the ecclesiastical discipline in order that these colleges might be a perpetual nursery of God's ministers."

But from the first centuries of the church, the popes and bishops had already cared for the formation of candidates to the priesthood in accord with Christ's command "to be the salt of the earth and the light of the world." The particular conditions concerning the way of finding ecclesiastical vocations, of choosing them and of watching over them, were given at the first and second councils of Toledo, in the sixth and seventh centuries, and by St. Gregory the Great, Honorius I, Leo III, and Innocent III.

The Council of Trent wanted to crown its magnificent work of restoring Catholic faith and morals by assuring a preparation of the clergy ever more worthy of its mission and always better conformed to its sacred dignity. A historian of the Council of Trent, Cardinal Pallavicino, affirmed that the work of the Council, which was prolonged over fifteen years in the midst of all kinds of difficulties, " would have been sufficiently rewarding had it been only for the seminaries which they gave to the church and which constituted the only means of having sacred discipline flourish."

The importance of the seminary, its function and exclusive purpose of preparing young men for the priesthood, have been sanctioned by the Code in canons 1354 to 1363. The Code takes the text of the Council of Trent almost verbatim: " that each diocese have in a fitting location, chosen by the bishop, its seminary or college in which, according to the possibilities and extent of the diocese, a certain number of young men will be prepared for the ecclesiastical state. Their character and will must offer hope that they will consecrate themselves forever and with fruit to the sacred ministry."

The preparation for the Second Ecumenical Council of the Vatican could not help considering seminaries in a special way, by studying their present situation and indispensable character, their ends and means, the duties of superiors, and the moral, intellectual, and physical qualities of its students. Leo XIII said of superiors in a letter to the bishops of Italy: " The personal conduct of the superior is the most eloquent and persuasive language to inculcate in the souls of young men a conviction of their duties and a love for good." The choice of a superior is one of the most delicate tasks of the bishop.

The church, in her maternal wisdom, knows that each vocation is like a seed that must find a fitting milieu in which to develop. This milieu is the seminary, be it diocesan, interdiocesan, or regional. There, a vocation is the object of the attentive care of priestly hearts, rich with the love of God, nourished with sacred science, matured with pastoral experience, with a great prudence, and learned in psychology and pedagogy.

When, in spite of the needs, a young man shows that he lacks the required qualities and does not have sufficient willpower to face the self-denial that the priesthood demands, superiors are obliged to dismiss him from the seminary, even if the lack of priests becomes greater daily, even if the needs of parishes are always more urgent. What counts in the work of God's Kingdom is not quantity but quality, to the extent that in the case of doubt it is better to run the risk of rejecting a probable vocation rather than to take the risk of confiding the care of a flock to a bad shepherd.

The formation of a candidate to the priesthood demands a long apprenticeship during which time from the sacramental life and prayer, especially liturgical prayer, the church strives to form a firm and true will, a pure and sure conscience, and an intelligence strengthened by knowledge and illumined by faith. Such again today are the tasks of every seminary. To attain such a level, study and prayer are naturally necessary, as well as discipline, a spirit of sacrifice, a love of the evangelical counsels, and the practice of abnegation. Errors can creep in here and there on these points. The pretext of these errors is often certain fashionable theories that propose a form of education left almost entirely to the free initiative and inclinations of each one. This phrase from the Gospel is valid in our day: " Every branch which bears fruit, the father prunes it, that it may bear even more fruit."

A seminary superior, having become a bishop, thus specified the role of a seminary to prepare priests for our time: " We could be tempted, speaking of the priests of tomorrow, to insist only upon the new condition of the priest in the new civilization. . . . But before being ' the priest of tomorrow,' he must be the priest of always. The servant priest of God, *Alter Christus,* is the minister of the Eucharistic sacrifice, the distributor of the mysteries of God for the mystical body, the sanctifier of souls by the sacraments, especially the sacrament of Penance, the minister of the word and the apostle of truth, the man of prayer and intercession. These sublime functions require of him great sanctity, chastity, disinterestedness, zeal for the glory of God and the salvation of souls, the spirit of discipline and obedience, and the knowledge of Christian faith and morals."

These principles have often been expressed by the Supreme Pontiffs, in particular: Pius X in *Haerent animo,* Pius XI in *Ad Catholici sacerdotii,* Pius XII in *Menti nostrae,* and John XXIII in his many discourses addressed to priests and seminarians, recalling the symbolic meaning of the books and chalice, i.e., of science and piety of doctrine, and the spirit of mortification.

June 13, 1962

THE PROBLEMS OF CATHOLIC SCHOOLS

The Central Commission continued this morning, June 13, the examination of a few schemata presented by Cardinal Pizzardo, president of the Commission on Studies and Seminaries, concerning Catholic schools and obedience to the magisterium in the teaching of the sacred sciences.

Teaching is one of the fundamental tasks of the church, ordered by the divine Master: " Go into the whole world and proclaim the good news to all creation." We must not think, as some pretend, that this mandate must be fulfilled by preaching alone or at least by catechetical teaching. The school is, in fact, the normal means not only of forming the intelligence but also of educating the heart. The church has the right to have her schools and to mobilize all her energies in order to inform the state schools with a Christian spirit. Pius XII said: " Every soul finds its salvation or ruin in school." Too much is at stake for the church to be indifferent to the school problem. Incalculable spiritual and moral values are at stake.

Schools, like seminaries, received a new and vigorous moral impetus from the Council of Trent. This Council founded new schools where there were none and restored strength to those already existing. The Council especially obligated priests to see that a serious and complete course be given to all, the poor as well as the rich, by truly competent masters, able to unite faith and profound wisdom. Thus they went back to the custom (never really abandoned by the church) of the church's educational solicitude, of teaching not only Christian doctrine but also every other subject from simple grammar to philosophy.

Answering the exhortations and degrees of the Council of Trent, dioceses and parishes, ancient institutes and new religious families, spared no effort to spread in all social classes and especially among the poor (at that time very much abandoned to ignorance) a religious instruction, the foundation and guide of all other knowledge. The years of the Council of Trent saw, alongside the Jesuits, who had just founded their colleges, the appearance of the Somasques and the Barnabites, who also opened places of learning. Finding themselves limited in this, the Scolopes and Brothers of the Christian Schools, to mention the more famous institutes of this period, also opened institutions in the field of education. A great apostle of Catholic schools as well as seminaries arose in the person of St. Charles Borromeo. He founded the university college in Pavia. His example was imitated by Cardinal Ghislieri, soon to become Pius V.

With the advent of humanism and laicism, the school, now separated from the church, took on an aspect that we call today nonconfessional, but that was in reality antireligious. Leo XIII said that "we could not imagine a more universal and efficacious means of divorcing society, the family, and individuals from the influence of the church and the faith" than lay schools. Pius XII also deplored the evil effect of the non-Christian school when he said: "Daily instruction, during the period of years, acts as a very captivating, slow but persisting, force, almost invisible, but for that reason so much more basic." Being inspired by this realistic conception of things, Pius XI masterfully set forth in the encyclical *Divini illius magistri* that the church felt compelled to defend with tireless vigilance and great doctrinal clarity the principles concerning the freedom of education while condemning contrary errors. Pius XII also brought out this deplorable state of affairs: "It is sad to note that in this domain . . . a long custom of state-dominated schools has obscured the very notion of the right to free education in the eyes of many," but nevertheless "the education of youth has never had such a decisive and vital importance as it has today. It is faced with the disconcerting errors of naturalism and materialism that invade the world."

In defending the freedom of the schools, the church also intends to defend the liberty of the family, upon which the first works of education are incumbent, as well as the liberty of the individual who cannot forget his natural end even in the choice of the human means for his intellectual perfection. The church is not content to remain on the defensive, but intends her schools and masters, who glory in the name of Christian, to be always equal to their task, because of their methods and programs, and equal to the seriousness of their studies and possessing a healthy modern spirit. The right to liberty entails duties of preparing and choosing educators, of surveillance over the programs and the formation of conscientious public opinion. The church seeks to organize always in view of better adapting to the needs and the education of the faithful, to harmonize their material and moral cooperation with their faith.

Let us mention, finally, this categoric statement of Pius

XII: " The See of Peter, the sentinel that cares over the good of souls and true progress, has never abdicated this essential right in the past. It has always admirably exercised it by means of its institutions, which were then the only ones consecrating themselves to this task. This see, moreover, will not abdicate this right in the future, neither for material gain nor out of fear of persecutions. This see will never allow the church to lose the effective exercise of its innate right which she has by divine right, or allow the family, which claims it by virtue of natural justice, to lose it. The faithful the world around witness the steadfastness with which the Apostolic See stands in the defense of school liberty in so many countries, and in the midst of very different circumstances and populations. For the school, as well as for worship and the holiness of matrimony, one must not hesitate to face all the difficulties and perils with the quiet conscience of one serving a just and holy cause. This cause is willed by God and has the certitude of rendering an inestimable service to civil society itself."

June 14, 1962

THE COLLABORATION OF RELIGIOUS INSTITUTES WITH THE PASTORAL MINISTRY OF BISHOPS

The schema presented today, June 14, is the result of a joint work by the Commission for Bishops and Diocesan Government and the Commission for Religious. The themes common to both were studied by a subcommission. The subject was presented under its twofold aspect by Cardinal Marella, speaking for the bishops and by Valerio Cardinal Valeri, speaking for religious.

In order to accomplish her teaching and sanctifying mission, the church needs the cooperation of secular and religious priests. Because their members are elevated to the dignity of the priesthood, they are to be the "wise cooperators" of the bishops, as is mentioned in the rite of ordination, and they are to aid the pastoral ministry of the bishop. The non-priest members of institutes of perfection have a greater duty than the laity to work with diligence and dedication for the growth of the mystical body of Christ.

This is why bishops have always sought the help of religious, especially today when ever-greater dangers menace the salvation of souls.

The first general task of religious is certainly prayer, penance, and reparation; but for many among them, the apostolate properly so called has been also added, according to the modes established by the different rules. This apostolate is in perfect unity with the bishops, to whom the divine right for the care of souls is confided, and in perfect collaboration with the diocesan clergy.

From these observations we can deduce certain principles concerning the jurisdiction and authority of the bishop in his diocese, the fidelity of religious to the ideals of their life and their apostolate, the rights of exemption, and the modes of collaboration between the diocesan and regular clergy.

All these questions are important. Many of them are treated clearly in the Code. But new exigencies and situations of these latter decades in the mission countries and elsewhere merit consideration, and must be regulated, inasmuch as possible, to favor the progress of religious in the way of perfection, the development of different orders and congregations, and the efficacy of the apostolate among the faithful.

THE EXEMPTION

The most important and interesting question from a juridical point of view is the one on exemption. It may be useful to see how it actually presents itself.

Exemption is a privilege by which some religious depend directly on the Holy See rather than on the bishop of the diocese where their community lives. This privilege, with all the different clauses foreseen by the Code, is granted for the greater good of the church. It places at the disposal of the supreme and universal authority persons and institutions that can exercise their beneficent activities on a wider scale. It is also granted for the greater good of the religious institutes that can then be developed in a more organic way, with an autonomy of structure and internal order more becoming to their vitality. The Supreme Pontiff, with full jurisdiction over the whole church, can then (because of the exemption) better dispose the important spiritual and moral forces represented by each religious family and place them at the service not only of the limited territorial needs of a diocese but in a truly panoramic and universal vision of the whole church.

The first examples of exemption, at least in embryonic form, date back to the end of the fourth century. Certain patriarchs of the Orient granted these to some monasteries which they took under their own direct authority, thus removing them from the jurisdiction of the bishop. It is in Rome, in 601, that we find the first example of an exemption, properly so called. During the course of a particular council at this time, the pope decided that " the tranquillity of monasteries " had to be respected by all, even by the bishop. The bishop could not give special orders to the monks, in order that " being separated from all inopportune trouble, they could fulfill their daily duty with greater devotion." In 628, Honorius I granted the exemption to the monastery of Bobbio. Pope Zachary granted it to the monastery of Monte Cassino in 741; Urban II, to Cava dei Tirreni in 1092; Alexander III to the monastery of Florence in 1176. In the twelfth century, almost all the monasteries had obtained the exemption. The new orders and congregations later followed their example; this, however, did not occur without some abuses. The Council of Constance, the Fourth Lateran, and finally the Council of Trent made restrictions. Trent in particular, without abolishing all the exemptions, decided to consider the question " with justice, truth, prudence, and equity." A general law, it said, should be promulgated to indicate the limits of the exemption, not to diminish the authority of the bishops. The Code of Canon Law later incorporated the decisions of the Council of Trent, also using pontifical documents dating back to Pius V in 1567, Gregory XV in 1622, Clement XII in 1735, Benedict XIV in 1742, 1744, and 1753, and Leo XIII in 1881.

To understand better the motives for the exemption of religious, let us cite the words of Pope John XXIII, addressed on March 25, 1960, to the superiors of institutes of perfection, participating in the Pontifical Commission's sessions for Latin America. The Holy Father certainly does not wish to speak about exemption, but he appeals for help from religious to face (in tight formation and in a regular and homogeneous fashion) the difficulties of these vast territories: " We must," he said, " assemble the holy energies of the church — the marvelous strength of the ancient religious orders; of the many institutes, congregations, and societies of perfection, for men and women; and the apostolate — and the most recent secular institutes, in order to orient them with an ever greater efficacy toward the vast horizons opening up to their benef-icent influence in these territories. We must, in fact, send personnel answering, as much as possible by their number, the needs of the great harvest that awaits. We must found new schools, new hospitals, asylums, and works of a social char-acter. We must, moreover, widen the context of existing activities, and above all we must be concerned with priestly and religious vocations."

The Holy Father added: " It is a universal appeal that concerns all, and obliges us to make our Divine Lord's redemp-tive work efficacious and lasting. He came into the world to do his Father's will. This explains our priestly mission and the pressing appeal for vocations. This is the meaning of the wonderful blossoming forth of both ancient and new religious families. These wish to prolong the salvific mission of the Son of God and to give him their aid through their various works and attributes.

" The history and character of your institutes, the unfolding of your activities in all domains of the church's life, your charity in teaching, and your mission of assistance — all these are concretely attested to by your effective and active presence in so many nations. To all this, we must add all you have done so far for the needs of Latin America. All has been done in a fervent spirit of collaboration and at the cost of real sacrifices. We wish to thank you most cordially for it."

CATHOLIC ASSOCIATIONS, MASS STIPENDS, LEGACIES, ORDINATION OF NON–CATHOLIC MINISTERS

Following the discussion on the relations of bishops and religious, three different schemata of decree were presented by Cardinal Ciriaci, the president of the Commission on the Discipline of the Clergy and the Christian People. The first was on Catholic associations; the second on Mass stipends and legacies for certain works; and the third was on the admission of non-Catholic ministers to sacred orders after conversion.

These are not new questions, but they may need revision to adapt them better to new circumstances. The Code treats these problems and provides for eventual modifications. The Central Commission examined these today for adoption by the Council or for study by the commission preparing the revision of the Code.

June 15, 1962

THE STATES OF PERFECTION

This morning, June 15, the Central Commission resumed work on the three schemata of decree presented at the end of yesterday's meeting by Cardinal Ciriaci. This ended the presentation of schemata by the Commission on the Discipline of the Clergy and the Christian People.

Valerio Cardinal Valeri immediately followed with the chapters not yet examined from a schema of the constitution prepared by the Commission for Religious, over which he presides. After his report, a discussion followed of the church's doctrine on the states of perfection and on the constitution uniting all the questions pertaining to the three kinds of states of perfection.

The words of Christ: " Be perfect as your heavenly Father is perfect," are the source from which many souls during the twenty centuries of Christianity have drawn strength to give up even the licit attractions of the world. They have consecrated their lives to an ideal of sanctity demanding the perfect and generous practice of the three evangelical vows: obedience, chastity, and poverty. Pius XI observed in his apostolic letter *Unigenitus Dei filius* that by these words: " If you want to be perfect, go, sell what you have; give it to the poor, and you will have a treasure in heaven; then, come, follow me," Jesus outlined a way of spiritual perfection to be taken by all who want to follow in his footsteps. Leo XIII also underscored this idea, writing to Cardinal Richard, archbishop of Paris, in 1900: " Everyone knows that religious orders originated and draw their meaning from these sublime evangelical counsels which our Divine Redeemer addressed to all who want to reach Christian perfection."

Naturally, the church has always fostered the development of religious vocations in many ways. Her solicitude is attested to by the many papal and conciliar documents directed toward securing the better observance of the rules and constitutions of each state of perfection. The Council of Trent, in particular, gave a new and vigorous impetus to religious life, along with an expansion of the most varied activities in education, the apostolate, and charitable and social works. This was done by maintaining and even strengthening the inherent obligations of personal sanctification according to the ideals of each order or congregation. Our epoch of great change and rapid evolution in uses and modes of life as well as of apostolic forms does, doubtless, demand new adaptations. These could lead to an efficacious evangelization with modern methods and to the spiritual enrichment of religious and their communities. As the Holy Father has often said, the Council is meant to be a means of general renewal and lasting invigoration for the whole church, in her human structures as well as in her instruments of expansion and defense. Religious also feel the time ripe for a renewal of their original spirit, by devoting themselves to the spiritual and psychological needs of modern men.

According to the present Code, there are three categories of states of perfection: the religious, properly so called, i.e., religious congregations and orders of clerics and laity; societies without vows; and secular institutes.

" Religious are ecclesiastical societies, erected, approved, and wisely organized by the church, by means of legislation general and particular (rules and constitutions), to afford the opportunity of professing the religious state of Christian perfection adequately and officially."

Societies of common life without vows are societies of ecclesiastics or laity who, without taking public vows, lead a common life to attain perfection and to consecrate themselves to apostolic work.

Secular institutes date back to the end of the eighteenth century, but were juridically recognized only in 1947. The members of these foundations do not wear a particular habit, they lead no common life according to canonical rules, they take no public vows, and finally, they retain their same social condition, priest or lay, after their consecration to the Lord. This social condition carries all the juridical and practical consequences that flow from it. By their obligatory practice of the three evangelical counsels, the members of secular institutes consecrate themselves to all forms of the apostolate corresponding to the exigencies of modern life.

These three categories have the very substance of the states of perfection in common, i.e., the perpetual practice and obligation of obedience, chastity, and poverty in an institute approved by ecclesiastical authority. They differ only in their manner of taking vows, of living out their ideal of perfection, and of exercising the activities inherent in their state according to rules, constitutions, and statutes proper to each of the three states of perfection.

The states of perfection are also equally distinct from the episcopal state and the state of the diocesan clergy.

The constitutive elements of the states of perfection were not juridically determined by the church in the early Christian era, but have developed slowly with the practice of communal life, starting with the monachism of the East and West. Then, due to the maturing experiences in other new forms of religious life that led to progress in canonical discipline, along with the theological and canonical doctrine, the constitutive elements of the religious life became fixed by the end of the Middle Ages. These elements were then defined and they perdured until 1900. At this time, Leo XIII introduced a fundamental innovation by his Constitution *Conditae a Christo,* by accounting the congregations with simple vows equal to the other religious families. A few years later, the Code of Canon Law took a further step by declaring congregations as a state of perfection, having the same juridical effects as the religious families. The Code also recognized a new state of evangelical perfection in the societies of common life without vows. Finally, Pius XII broadened the concept of the state of perfection by his Constitution *Provida mater ecclesia* of 1947; he included therein, with some reservations, secular institutes.

Because of the different forms of states of perfection, we can say that the church offers her many children of both sexes the opportunity of choosing a mode of life best suited to each one's gifts, ideals, and vocation. Be it in the active apostolate or in the silence of contemplation, she provides a response to all the spiritual and material needs of the human race. One must guard, however, against an excessive activity reducing and even stifling the interior spirit of prayer and the life of study. One must equally deny oneself an apostolate or a charitable work that would not be totally supernatural. Pius XII said: " Beneficence that springs not from faith but from some other human motive is not charity, and cannot be called Catholic. Charity has a dignity, a breath, and a force that is lacking in simple philanthropy, regardless of the means and works undertaken."

Finally, let us recall certain fundamental truths: the state of perfection certainly represents a higher and more generous ideal, one dearer to God, than the state of matrimony. It must certainly not be considered as a convenient way of escaping from the difficulties of life. It imposes serious and constant sacrifices. Although involving a very high ideal filled with self-denial and difficulties, it must not be considered impossible for a Christian in good faith and having complete confidence in the grace of the Lord.

With the end of this morning's discussion, all the schemata prepared by the Commission for Religious have been examined.

June 16, 1962

DISPOSITIONS REQUIRED FOR
SACRED ORDERS

The Central Commission today, Saturday, June 16, examined, during the first part of the session, two schemata on the required preparation for the reception of the sacraments of Orders and Marriage. They were presented by Cardinal Aloisi Masella, the president of the Commission on the Discipline of the Sacraments.

The priestly dignity, making a man a minister of God and a father of souls, is so exalted that it requires, insofar as is humanly possible, perfect purity of morals and sanctity of life. The Roman Pontiff reminded the young men to be ordained of the obligation to be " pure and chaste " if they wanted to become worthy dispensers of the mysteries of God.

The insistence of the Supreme Pontiffs on certain principles of priestly asceticism clearly indicates the fundamental need for the priest, who wants to have a fruitful ministry, of an eminent practice of all the Christian virtues. Let us mention especially these documents of the past sixty years: St. Pius X, in the exhortation *Haerent animo;* Pius XI, in the encyclical *Ad Catholici sacerdotii;* Pius XII, in the exhortation *Menti nostrae;* and John XXIII in the allocution to the clergy during the first Roman Synod.

Precisely because of the very grave responsibilities before God and men imposed by the priesthood, the preparation for the sacrament of Orders must receive the highest care. The Council of Trent obliged bishops to examine candidates with great attention. Men to be admitted to Orders must show evidence, inasmuch as possible, that they are " so pious and firm in chastity that one can hope for good example during their entire lives."

This preliminary examination gives knowledge to superiors and the bishop himself about the young men to be ordained. It presupposes a few years of apprenticeship to acquire the solid virtue to resist the shock experienced by the young priest in his lifelong priestly apostolate in the midst of an attractive world ever solicitous of evil. Chastity, furthermore, is not a self-sustaining virtue; it must be nourished with piety and charity.

In his encyclical *Ad Catholici sacerdotii,* Pius XI underlines the need for piety: " Without piety, the most holy practices and the most august rites of the sacred ministry will be mechanically performed in a routine way. They will lack spirit, unction, and life. Also, venerable brothers, the piety we speak of is not that false piety which is inconsistent, superficial, and self-satisfying but does not nourish; one that flatters but does not sanctify. It is, rather, that solid piety which does not succumb to the incessant fluctuations of sentiment but rests on the principles of the surest doctrine. It consists in solid convictions that resist the assaults and seductions of temptation."

In turn, Pope John XXIII, in his allocution at the second session of the Roman Synod, recalled the beneficent influence of charity: "To forestall the weaknesses of the heart and to correct them from disastrous consequences, St. Peter speaks and continues to exhort the heart of priests to practice charity as a guarantee against the grave pitfalls to which the weakness of the senses lead."

THE REQUIRED DISPOSITIONS FOR THE SACRAMENT OF MARRIAGE

The great dignity of the sacrament of Marriage also demands that the spouses prepare for it with great care. This must be done not only to make its celebration licit and valid but especially to make it spiritually fruitful.

In marriage a man and woman begin a new life with new duties and lasting reciprocal commitments. These are in the unity, indissolubility, and fecundity of a contract elevated to the dignity of a sacrament. There can be, therefore, no levity in this matter. It should not be contracted out of passion or caprice. What is in question, along with the human happiness of the spouses and their children, is eternal salvation itself. Pius XI observed in the encyclical *Casti connubii:* "One cannot deny that the solid foundation of a happy marriage and the ruin of an unhappy one is already prepared in the souls of youth from childhood and adolescence. For one fears that those who egotistically sought themselves in all things and abandoned themselves to their lust before marriage will act the same in marriage as they did before marriage. One also fears that they will reap what they have sown, i.e., a sad family life, with tears, mutual hatred, quarrels, misunderstandings, contempt for common life, and above all, will still find themselves with uncontrolled passions."

Pastors, therefore, and all shepherds of souls must instruct, educate, and form in youth a Christian view of life, and lead them to consider marriage in its true reality, as involving responsibilities, errors, and difficulties, and show them the means, with grace, which will help youth to surmount them. It requires long and patient preparation, which must be done, as much as possible, by the pastor with a broad mind and a zealous heart. It is a catechetical, juridical, and pastoral preparation. The pastor has the further grave obligation of examining the spouses, and not only of investigating possible obstacles to the licit and valid celebration of the marriage but also of finding out whether they are spiritually prepared to take this great step.

One must also note this passage from the encyclical *Casti connubii:* " As all must be referred to the law and to God's mind to have the perduring restoration of marriage verified everywhere, in like manner, it is of greatest importance that the faithful be well instructed about marriage, by written and oral teaching, not only once lightly in passing but frequently and solidly. Clear and convincing arguments should be given so that these truths may vitally seize their mind and penetrate to the depths of their hearts."

June 18, 1962

THE APOSTOLATE OF THE LAITY

After the brief Sunday rest, the Central Commission resumed work under the presidency of Cardinal Tisserant. It examined this morning, June 18, a long schema on the Constitution for Apostolate of the Laity, presented by Fernando Cardinal Cento. This subject has long been awaited because of the new aspects that may flow from it. In its study of the various sections of the schema, the Central Commission proved its appreciation of the rightful importance of the layman's ever growing and better coordinated contribution to the church's work in the world, that of leading all souls to salvation.

The Commission for Laymen faced a difficult task. It had to map out a new course on many points, not only in formulating definitions for clearer doctrinal understanding (this was not its function), but in ordering the abundant material especially from the pontifical documents of the last few decades. It had to present the organic ways in which the laity can become the gospel leaven in modern society. This leaven is able to ferment the multiple activities of modern men with the Christian spirit. For these reasons, the Commission divided its work into three distinct sections, preceded by a foreword recalling the general principles applicable to each activity studied: to Apostolic Action properly so called, or Catholic Action, according to the different forms in each country; to Charitable Action; and to Social Action. This is a panorama of vast dimensions which could not be explored under all its innumerable aspects. It could be studied, however, in the light of the church's traditional doctrine, along with the directives of the recent pontifical teachings. This field of action can be made more precise according to the needs and situations that are gradually developing.

The words of Jesus are as a heart's lament: " Other sheep I have who are not of this fold; we must lead them to it. They, then, will hear my voice and there will be but one flock under the direction of one shepherd." These words have always awakened a desire in the heart of the most faithful for a generous apostolate in collaboration with the hierarchy and according to its directives. One who truly loves God experiences the urgent need to make him known and loved by his brothers also. One who understands the value of grace cannot but strive in every way to have those he meets at home, at work, and in society participate in this gift. One who is conscious of the meaning and effects of the sacraments, especially Baptism and Confirmation, feels an urgent need in his heart to be like Christ and to witness Christ in all his actions.

This he does even in the secular field by radiating " the sweet odor of Christ " and by working for the *consecratio mundi,* the consecration of the world, the family, the profession, the school, and the state.

Pius XI stressed this essential aspect of the apostolate in a letter to the Argentinean episcopacy in 1931: " Whoever loves God can do no less than have all love him; whoever truly loves his neighbor can do no less than desire his eternal salvation, and work to secure it for him. This is the foundation upon which the apostolate is based. This is nothing else than the exercise of Christian charity which obliges all men."

The apostolate of laymen is not a new phenomenon in the church. One need only read The Acts of the Apostles, the persecutions of the first centuries, and the history of the church to become aware of this. In our times, however, when so many activities of the temporal order have been emptied of all spiritual idealism, making the natural order an irreducible contradiction of the supernatural, a new fervor has arisen among believers to renew all the manifestations of life with a Christian mind, spirit, and appearance. The hierarchy and its priests have become more and more engaged in this vast work of evangelization. They have had to face ever-growing spiritual needs while also facing the questions of population, missionary development, the bitterness and anxieties of a world frustrated by its own self-confidence, and always incapable of finding peace and equilibrium outside the law of God. From this situation, the need has arisen for laymen who are aware of their place and duties in the church, conscious especially of their duty to live and think with the church. These laymen make the church's problems theirs, and participate, as much as possible, in her mission of bringing light and salvation. They are ready to place their professional gifts, talents, experience, and especially their faith, lived hour by hour in their personal, family, and social life, at the service of the church.

A mandate from the hierarchy is necessary when the exercise of the apostolate, properly so called, is added to the apostolate of witnessing one's faith in one's work. The hierarchy, then, assumes responsibility for it. Priests have the duty of forming the laity for the apostolate and of giving them spiritual direction. The laity, on the other hand, must organize themselves under the hierarchy to study the best means of realizing an effective apostolate, according to the needs, conditions, and mentalities of each country. They must be animated by the spirit of faith alone and the desire to serve the church, in perfect union of intention, with all the other apostolic associations. These associations may differ in their immediate ends but really converge, for their purpose is the same, i.e., to help the church save souls. There will be, then, some organizations set up to spread Christian doctrine by catechetical teaching or by other means of formation, e.g., the press, education, audio-visual means. Others will dedicate themselves to the bringing back of those who have strayed away from the faith, to the converting of infidels, or to the transforming of the church's enemies by a gradual penetration of Christian principles. Others, moreover, will help in the Liturgical Apostolate, the Social Apostolate, and by works of charity, to mention only these examples.

We may then speak of a family apostolate for a better preparation of youth for marriage and to help the often insufficient Christian formation of children. We may also speak of an apostolate in the instruction and education of children and adolescents, of an apostolate among laborers and professionals, among urban and rural dwellers. This is done by adapting the apostolate to the idiom, mentality, and spiritual needs of each group. The apostolate also extends into international and supranational circles by means of a special preparation to cope with the most diverse of problems and to offer a Christian solution to them. We can speak of an apostolate set up to create and establish a climate of understanding and union with our separated brothers, and again of an apostolate established for the missions or for the return to the church of great multitudes dechristianized by materialism and laicism, and finally, an apostolate to review art, culture, mores, entertainment, spectacles, and the different aspects of contemporary society.

We can also consider as an apostolate the one exercised on the plane of charity; it is, however, under forms and with means different from the multiform apostolate mentioned above. There is, moreover, an apostolate on the social, economic, and political levels, although based on different relationships with the hierarchy. Their purpose is to have the principles of the Christian social doctrine penetrate among men and institutions, into laws and the world of work, into the school and international organisms, into the use of new techniques and the administration of the common good. Since the gospel was not meant for individuals alone, but for society as well, its spirit should impregnate all the aspects of life (from family to the civic community, from the structures of each state to the federal, international, and worldwide structures) with the ferment of justice and charity, by the work of dedicated and united Christians. This capillary diffusion alone, and its universal penetration of Christian principles, can guarantee real progress and a lasting peace among nations.

Aware of her mission to save each man for eternity, the church knows her duty to use the human means at her disposal, without divorcing man from the world in which he lives. By sanctifying him in the society he shares, she also sanctifies the society itself through the action of her best sons.

This morning's discussion continued on this unique and weighty schema on the apostolate of the laity until the subject was thoroughly completed.

THE MAGISTERIUM OF THE CHURCH IN SACRED SCIENCES

Jesus Christ gave the church, his spouse, the deposit of faith, and established her as the infallible teacher of divine truths. For this reason, whoever wishes to teach in the church and with the church must hold what she holds above all else. Pius XII said: " This certainly does not hinder theologians and scholars in their quest for the scientific foundation of a whole series of crucial questions of life. It is also certain that the Holy See loves, praises, and encourages scholarly research and the other speculations of theologians who penetrate revealed truths and do not hesitate to consider, explain, and support the declaration of the ecclesiastical magisterium with scientific rigor, in the light of reason and guided by faith, i.e., as Pius IX affirmed it in *In sensu ecclesiae.*"

One must be mindful, however, that " theologians exercise their functions, not by divine right, but from a delegation of the church; they remain, therefore, subject to the authority and vigilance of the legitimate magisterium. . . . What is decisive for the knowledge of truth is the *Sensus ecclesiae,* not the opinion of theologians. One would, otherwise, make theologians a kind of *magistri magisterii,* which would be an obvious error."

One must first of all teach the truth according to the church's doctrine, and then the errors that are contrary to it. In treating errors, the teacher must examine whether they come from a false principle or from an undue application of a just principle, from a defect in method or from an inadequate study of the problem. After this examination, he must show the content of the errors and strive to refute them for his students.

An instruction of the Biblical Commission recommends: " The professor will never forget that it is to the church that God has given not only the care of Sacred Scripture but also the task of interpreting it. It must, then, be explained only in the name of the church and in her spirit."

Concerning the studies of philosophy and theology, we must recall canon 1366, which says that St. Thomas Aquinas is the master from whom we are to seek the methods, doctrine, and principles of these sciences. This was what the Holy Father, John XXIII, said in a discourse to seminary superiors: " Before all, a solid Christian philosophical formation is had according to the principles, doctrine, and method of St. Thomas Aquinas. He gives to the modern student and to the man of tomorrow a balanced judgment, profound views, good sense, and intellectual maturity. It is in the light of these clarifying principles that one can judge the true value of vast movements in culture, literature, modern thought, and the lacunae and dangers of the technological spirit."

The presentation of these schemata to the Central Commission brought the preparatory work of the Commission on Studies and Seminaries to a close.

June 19, 1962

THE MAGISTERIUM
AND THE AUTHORITY OF THE CHURCH

Cardinal Ottaviani inaugurated the works of this morning's meeting (June 19) by presenting the second part of the constitution schema on the church. The first part of this schema had been discussed during Session VI, last May. These chapters as well as the preceding ones are rich in theological doctrine. They concern the magisterium and the church's authority, the church-state relations, the church's duty and need to announce the gospel to all peoples, and ecumenism in the church. The works were presided over by Cardinal Micara, the vicar of His Holiness for the diocese of Rome.

According to the expression of St. Paul, the church is " the pillar and foundation of truth " and has received from her Founder the promise of indefectible assistance from the Holy Spirit. While preserving her teaching from all error, the Holy

Spirit helps her to preserve faithfully the deposit of revelation, which was closed at the death of the last apostle, St. John.

There is, then, in the church a living, perpetual, and authentic magisterium whose task is to teach the truth in the name of Christ: "Who hears you hears me; who despises you despises me." It is not, therefore, the doctrine of a man, no matter how learned and wise he may be, which is set forth by the Roman Pontiff when he defines and condemns in the fullness of his authority ex cathedra. Nor is the view expressed by the bishops united with the pope during an ecumenical council the simple opinion of an assembly. In both cases, Christ speaks through Peter and the apostles in communion with him. In both cases, the Holy Spirit manifests his light, not only to preserve the integrity of the deposit of faith, but also to make it more clearly known through the progress of studies.

The church could not fail in this task of guarding and teaching the truth, regardless of the promises or menaces of the hopes of success or of imminent peril. Leo XIII said in the encyclical *Libertas* of June 20, 1888: " In what concerns faith and morals, God made the church participate in his divine magisterium and gave her the divine privilege of not knowing error. This is why she is the great and sure teacher of men and possesses the inviolable right to teach freely. And, in fact, finding her own support in her heavenly teachings, the church has always desired to fulfill religiously this God-given mission. Never allowing herself to be intimidated by the difficulties that surround her on every side, she has never ceased to defend the freedom of her magisterium."

The faithful must give their religious adherence of intellect and will to the magisterium of the Roman Pontiff, even when he does not speak ex cathedra. The pope's intention and will, the indication of the documents themselves, and other expressions of the same doctrine, are all criteria to be used. The mind and will of the Supreme Pontiffs are principally manifested by the doctrinal acts that concern the whole church. These are, for example, certain Apostolic Constitutions, encyclicals, and at times certain particularly important allocutions. These principal documents of the ordinary magisterium of the church usually contain traditional doctrine which is further clarified and refined.

On the question of obedience to the magisterium of the Supreme Pontiff, Leo XIII said in his encyclical *Sapientiae christianae* of January 10, 1890: " When we delineate the limits of obedience owed to pastors of souls, and especially to the Roman Pontiff, we must not think only of dogmas to be intellectually adhered to lest one commit the crime of heresy. . . . Among the elements of revelation, some refer to God, the principle of the beatitude we hope for, and others refer to man and to the means of attaining this beatitude. It belongs by divine right to the church, and in the church to the Roman Pontiff, to determine in both these orders what must be believed and what must be done. This is why the Pontiff must be able to judge with authority what the Word of God contains, to decide what doctrines are in harmony with it, and which ones contradict it. Likewise, in the field of morals it is his task to determine what is right and what is wrong, what must be done and what must be avoided if one wishes to attain eternal salvation. Otherwise, he could neither be the infallible interpreter of the Word of God, nor the sure guide of human life."

If we look upon the authority of the pope and the bishops with the eyes of faith, it is easy to perceive Christ himself in it and to obey " in simplicity of heart, as to Christ; not by a purely external obedience seeking to please men, but as slaves of Christ who fulfill the will of God with spirit." These words of St. Paul preserve their full vigor, although they were written nineteen hundred years ago to the Christians of Ephesus.

CHURCH AND STATE

Along with the authority of the church, there is her power. This power extends to everything relevant to the eternal salvation of souls. As Leo XIII writes in his encyclical *Immortale Dei* of November 1, 1885: "Everything in human affairs is sacred by some title, either bearing on the salvation of souls or on divine cult by its nature or in relation to its purpose."

Politics can be included among those aspects of life which can have a considerable indirect influence on the faith and spiritual welfare of individuals and peoples. Pius XII said: "Whenever it [politics] touches the other, then religion, the church, and her representative, the pope, have not only the right but also the duty to give indications and directives which Catholics have the right to demand and the duty to follow."

On the other hand, whatever tends by its nature to the temporal well-being of men belongs to civil authority. The church, although jealous of her rights, equally respects the rights of others and does not meddle in questions that do not concern her, provided, naturally, that the divine law be safeguarded. As for those questions which concern both the supernatural welfare of the church as well as the natural end of the state (e.g., marriage, the education of youth, etc.), the church only asks that she be not prevented from obtaining her own end, that the superior goods of the soul be not ignored, and that they be not sacrificed for interests of a secondary value.

Leo XIII also said: "God has divided the government of the human race between two powers, the ecclesiastical and the civil powers. The former is placed over divine affairs, the latter over human affairs. Each one is supreme in its own domain. Each one is enclosed within perfectly determined limits which are drawn in conformity with its nature and special end. There is, then, as it were, a circumscribed sphere within which each one exercises its action by its own right (*jure proprio*)."

Finally, civil authority cannot be indifferent to religion, much less opposed to it, if it does not want to impede the complete good of its citizens, for citizens have not only a body but a soul as well. From the wealth of pontifical teaching on this subject, let us quote the encyclical *Immortale Dei:* " States cannot, without impiety, rule as if God did not exist, or treat religion as a strange phenomenon (with no importance) by indifferently adopting one among many. On the contrary, they have the obligation to honor God in the way he himself showed he wanted to be honored."

RELIGIOUS LIBERTY

Side by side with the question of church and state, the question on religious liberty was presented by Cardinal Bea. The schema was prepared by the Secretariat for Christian Unity. The religious liberty, which the church claims, is not only freedom of opinion or the free performance of religious ceremonies; it is, rather, the ability to practice and proclaim all the private and public duties concerning God and men.

In the light of what has already been said, we can better understand canon 1322 of the Code, which says: " Independent of all civil power, the church has the right and the duty to teach the gospel to all men."

Tomorrow's work will continue on the ecumenism schema. It will be presented by the Theological Commission. Other schemata prepared by the Secretariat for Christian Unity will also be presented.

June 16, 1962

UNITY OF THE CHURCH

During the second part of the June 16 meeting, the Central Commission heard Cardinal Cicognani, president of the Commission for the Oriental Churches, report on a schema on the unity of Christians, seen uniquely from the aspect of the Oriental Churches. A vote was taken after the discussion.

The church is the mystical body of Christ. She is the society of the elect who are united in Christ and who obtain salvation in him.

There is a double aspect to the church: on the one hand, she is already triumphant with Christ, as the spouse of this spotless Lamb; on the other hand, the church is still engaged in the world. Here she must continue to use human social structures, to deal with temporal problems, to repel the assaults of error and corruption, in a word, of evil under all its forms. It is this earthly and temporal aspect of the church which necessitates laws and penalties, authority and jurisdiction, the hierarchy and the different grades, between superiors and inferiors.

Wanting to provide a solid and visible source of edification for his church on earth, Christ entrusted her to his ministers. To his apostles and especially to Peter, he gave the mission of directing and governing her. The visible unity of the church has its center in Peter and his successors, who govern, rule, and judge in the name of Christ and as his vicars. This unity can be safeguarded only if all the faithful on earth submit to this authority constituted by Christ, i.e., to the pope and the bishops united to Rome.

Unity, however, does not imply uniformity. It is praiseworthy to admit a diversity that respects the individual traditions, customs, and needs of a people and region. But especially in this case, a unique coordinating authority is necessary to unite all the faithful.

Unfortunately, the divisions that have come up in the church through the centuries have caused damage to souls. There was the need, then, to try all means, both natural and supernatural, to bring the scattered back to the one fold, whose invisible shepherd is Christ and whose visible one is Peter. Only in this way could Christ's prayer be realized: " Father, make them all one! "

The supernatural means is essentially prayer, by which humanly impossible tasks are made possible by the grace of God.

On the other hand, the human means can be many, ranging from the theological to the juridical, from the disciplinary to the psychological and practical.

These are certainly great problems which cannot be easily solved. For the moment, however, we can only repeat the prayer of St. Basil: " O Lord, make divisions cease in the church; reunite those who have scattered, bring back the strayed, to join them all to your holy, catholic, and apostolic church."

Having completed these schemata, the Commission on the Discipline of the Sacraments and the Commission for the Oriental Churches ended the presentation of their work.

June 20, 1962

ECUMENISM

After the Holy Father's visit and allocution on Wednesday, June 20, the Central Commission resumed its work under the presidency of Cardinal Micara. It continued the examination of chapters from the schema on the church already presented by Cardinal Ottaviani, president of the Theological Commission. The problem of ecumenism was studied first from a theological viewpoint; then Cardinal Bea set forth another schema on the same subject but from a pastoral point of view.

This meeting lasted into the afternoon in order to examine all the schemata called for by the order of the day.

Among the questions preoccupying the church, there is the one on the division that has arisen through the centuries in the unity of those who believe in Christ. One of the most pressing recommendations Jesus made to his apostles before his passion remains still without echo from a large number who nonetheless glory in the name Christian. Faced with this painful reality, the church has never ceased to intervene among persons and dissident Christian communities to help them rediscover the road to the Father's house. She has also always favored every effort made to inspire souls with thoughts and desires of true unity. She is, therefore, happy to see the ecumenical movement growing every day; and she wants to bring her aid not only by prayer and the goodwill of all who seek unity, but further, to encourage all theological and pastoral works destined to have the center of unity shine forth more clearly.

Great prudence is required in this question in order not to yield to impulses, perhaps generous in themselves but nonetheless not always enlightened. Erroneous forms of religious indifferentism, interconfessionalism, and even compromise must not make the present state of affairs worse, rather than improve it. The so-called irenic ecumenism is, in fact, much different from the true unity that Christ willed and recommended.

As we know, the word " ecumenical," as it is used today by non-Catholics and especially by Protestants, indicates a sort of relaxation, a kind of federation with equal rights of all the Christian churches. According to this theory, the different churches should consider themselves equally culpable for the separation. No one church could claim to be the one and only true church of Christ, but only one of its parts. The future church, resulting from the union of the diverse churches now in existence, would not be identical with any one of them, but would be completely new. It was on these suppositions that the pan-Christian assemblies met at Edinburgh in 1910, Stockholm in 1925, Lausanne in 1927, Oxford in 1937. The Catholic Church could naturally not adhere to these presuppositions. In 1946, the World Council of Churches was established. It held its first meeting in Amsterdam in 1948; its second in Evanston (U.S.A.) in 1954; and its third in New Delhi in November, 1961. The proceedings of this last meeting were attended by Roman Catholic observers. In his encyclical *Orientalis Ecclesiae* of 1944, Pius XII observed: " The method by which only main doctrines are agreed upon by choice and adopted does not lead to true and just unity in Christ. It is, rather, the method that gives place to all the divinely revealed truths in their integrity that offers the foundation of concord and agreement for Christ's faithful."

The Catholic Church, however, did not wait for the Protestant ecumenical movement to seek out every possible way to union. The Second Council of Lyons, and the Councils of Florence and Trent, show the church's effort to strive for Christ's ideal of one flock under the care of one shepherd. Monsignor Ragazzoni, the bishop of Nazianzus, spoke in these terms at the Council of Trent concerning the brothers who had refused to take part: " As things stand, it would have been highly desirable that these questions in the order of the day, especially favorable to them, be treated together with them. In their absence, however, we made their integrity and salvation our concern in such a way that it would not have been possible to do better with their presence. . . . For a long time, we have prepared the necessary remedy for their health; but if the sickness is to leave them, the medicine must spread through the veins into the whole body."

In more recent times, Pius IX in his letter *Arcano divinae Providentiae consilio* of September, 1868, cordially invited the " Orthodox " bishops to the First Council of the Vatican; on September 13 of the same year, he notified the Protestants of the Council in terms of sincere and paternal affection, in the letter *Jam vos omnes;* he did not, however, invite them.

Leo XIII gave a new impetus to the movement within the Catholic Church of studying the possibilities of union, especially with the Oriental Churches. He was cautious, meanwhile, to avoid whatever could be offensive or could create a still deeper division.

In 1909, a convert from Episcopalianism, Rev. Paul Wattson, began the unity octave with the approval of St. Pius X. A conference was later formed for all Catholics who had for many years consecrated their lives to ecumenical problems. Their twofold purpose was: to gather together the experience of all who study these questions of unity, and to establish, as much as possible, new rapports based on mutual confidence with the separated brothers.

This program was similar to the one started in the Secretariat for the Union of Christians by the Holy Father, John XXIII, when he said: "Also to show our love and benevolence to those who bear the name of Christ, but are separated from this Apostolic See, and in order that they may follow the works of the Council and find the way more easily to that unity for which Jesus addressed such an ardent prayer to his heavenly Father, we establish a special 'council' or secretariat, presided over by a cardinal to be chosen by us and to be organized as was indicated for the Commissions."

MARY, MOTHER OF GOD AND MEN

The Theological Commission presented a schema on the Blessed Virgin, the mother of God and of men. It was meant to unite the two schemata on ecumenism. Let us mention here that the Second Vatican Council will begin precisely on the feast of the maternity of Mary.

In the bull *Ineffabilis Deus* of December 8, 1854, Pius IX said: " We firmly hope and have complete confidence that the Blessed Virgin would want, by her powerful intercession, all separated Christians to return to us. This would be the road of truth and justice, after all doubts have been removed. There would then be one flock and one shepherd."

Now, John XXIII makes the meaning of Catholic Marian devotion very explicit, in order to prevent certain objections from our separated brothers. He says: " At the side of Jesus stands his mother Mary. Our filial sentiments are turned with confidence and affection toward such a mother for whom Catholics nourish the highest and deepest devotion. Some have criticized this sentiment in the past, as if it were an act of adoration due to God alone. But Catholics clearly venerate the mother of Jesus with enthusiasm, recognizing in her the prerogatives of being the mother of the Son of God made man.

While being the recipient of gifts from the Lord and inter-cessory power, she remains on earth a creature who is closer to God. . . . May we always have Jesus in our hearts; he is the source of courage, consolation, and every comfort. And at the same time, let us always have the image of Mary be-fore us."

SCHEMATA PRESENTED BY CARDINAL BEA

The other schemata prepared by the Secretariat for Chris-tian Unity and presented to the Commission by Cardinal Bea concern the following subjects: the necessity of prayer in order to obtain the grace from God to reunite the separated groups with the ever-living and vigorous mainstream of the church; the importance of the word of God as an instrument given to educate Christian people in order that a need for unity may be developed in them and cause them to act accordingly; and the church's desire to communicate the benefits of redemption to all men.

With the examination of these themes, the seventh and last session of the Central Commission came to a close. The fol-lowing groups still have work to do before the Council opens; the commission for technical organization; the three subcom-mittees on rules, amendments, and mixed matters. These sub-committees were constituted last November 7 within the Cen-tral Commission.

RECAPITULATION OF THE WORKS
OF THE CENTRAL COMMISSION

After the last session, the *Notiziaro* of the press service for the Central Commission recapitulated the works of the Cen-tral Commission, on June 23, in these terms:

In the course of the six sessions of November 1961, January, February, March-April, May, and June 1962, 70 schemata in 119 leaflets, totaling 2,060 pages, were examined.

The Central Commission examined 6 schemata of constitutions on: the sources of revelation, the moral order, the deposit of faith, chastity and the family, the church, and Mary, the mother of God and men. These were all prepared by the Theological Commission and presented by Cardinal Ottaviani. These schemata were contained in 23 leaflets and were examined during the November, January, May, and June sessions.

The Commission for Bishops and Diocesan Government studied 6 schemata contained in 9 leaflets. They were on: the main pastoral questions, the boundaries of dioceses, episcopal conferences, the relations between bishops and the Roman Curia, the auxiliary and coadjutor bishops. These projects were presented to the Central Commission by Paolo Cardinal Marella during the February and May sessions. A schema on the relations between bishops and religious was added in June. This schema was prepared by a mixed subcommission composed of members from the Commission for Bishops, and some from the Commission for Religious.

Seventeen schemata of decree, in as many leaflets, were examined by the Commission for the Discipline of the Clergy and the Christian People. These were on: the redistribution and sanctity of the clergy, the habit and tonsure, provision for parishes, the duties of pastors, ecclesiastical offices and benefices, the historic and artistic patrimony of the church, the catechism, the associations of the faithful, Mass stipends, pious donations, and the ordination of converted non-Catholic ministers. These themes were presented by Cardinal Ciriaci, and were discussed during the November, February, May, and June sessions.

The Commission for Religious presented a schema of constitution, divided into several parts and sections in 11 leaflets, on the states of perfection. Valerio Cardinal Valeri presented each part during the February, May, and June sessions.

The Commission for the Discipline of the Sacraments examined 9 schemata in 9 leaflets, presented by Cardinal Masella during the January, May, and June sessions. They were on the sacraments of: Orders, Confirmation, Penance, and Matrimony. This latter sacrament was studied in the aspects of its preparation and form of celebration, its impediments, and the consent of the spouses. Matrimonial trials and mixed marriages were also studied.

There was only one schema of constitution for the liturgy, composed of 8 chapters in 5 leaflets. It was elaborated under the presidency of Gaetano Cardinal Cicognani, and was presented during the March-April session by Cardinal Larraona after Cardinal Cicognani died.

The Commission on Studies and Seminaries presented 3 schemata of decree in 6 leaflets, and 2 schemata of constitution in 6 leaflets. They were on: priestly vocations, obedience to the ecclesiastical magisterium, university studies, Catholic schools, and the formation of seminarians. Cardinal Pizzardo reported them during the February and June sessions.

The Commission for the Oriental Churches examined 11 schemata of decree in as many leaflets. Amleto Cardinal Cicognani made the presentation during the January, February, May, and June sessions. The themes were: sacraments, rites and precepts of the Oriental Churches, patriarchs, relations with the separated brothers in acts of worship, vernacular, powers of bishops, catechism, celebration of Easter, divine office, and church unity.

The Commission on the Missions presented 7 schemata of decree in as many leaflets. Cardinal Agagianian made the presentation during the March-April session. They were on: life in the missions, the discipline of the clergy, religious missionaries, the liturgy, the discipline of Christians, studies in seminaries, and missionary cooperation.

The Commission on the Lay Apostolate presented its work in a report by Cardinal Cento during the June session. There was 1 schema of constitution composed of three parts and contained in 4 leaflets. The parts were: general notions; religious, charitable, and social action of the laity.

Likewise for the Secretariat for the Press and Entertainment, Bishop O'Connor presented, during the March-April session, 1 schema of constitution in two parts and subdivided under various titles. It was contained in 6 leaflets. Its theme was the different sectors of the media of social communication, i.e., the press, the cinema, radio, and television.

The Secretariat for Christian Unity presented 4 schemata of decree in as many leaflets during the June session. They were on: Catholic ecumenism, the necessity of praying for unity, the word of God as means of unity, and religious liberty. On this last-mentioned schema, the Secretariat treated especially the right of man to follow the exigencies of his own well-informed conscience, even in religious matters. Man also has the right and duty which flow from the following of conscience while living in civil society or in the state. In other words, the state has the duty in practice of respecting this right of its citizenry. This question was opened by Pius XII in his celebrated discourse to Catholic jurists on December 6, 1953. As we can see, this was a burning issue for our modern pluralistic society, and also extremely difficult. Cardinal Bea reported these schemata to the Central Commission.

APPENDIX I

LIST OF COMMISSIONS AND SECRETARIATS

Pope John's Apostolic Constitution of June 5, 1960, established the Preparatory Commissions for the Council. There were ten Commissions and two Secretariats. The Commissions were:

1. Commission on Theology, headed by Alfredo Cardinal Ottaviani.
2. Commission for Bishops and Diocesan Government, headed by Marcello Cardinal Mimmi; later Paolo Cardinal Marella.
3. Commission on Ecclesiastical Discipline and the Christian People, headed by Pietro Cardinal Ciriaci.
4. Commission for Religious, headed by Valerio Cardinal Valeri.
5. Commission on the Discipline of the Sacraments, headed by Benedetto Cardinal Aloisi Masella.
6. Commission on the Liturgy, headed by Gaetano Cardinal Cicognani; later, Arcadio Cardinal Larraona.
7. Commission on Seminaries and Catholic Universities, headed by Giuseppe Cardinal Pizzardo.
8. Commission for the Oriental Churches, headed by Amleto Cardinal Cicognani.
9. Commission on the Missions, headed by Gregory Peter Cardinal Agagianian.
10. Commission on the Lay Apostolate, headed by Fernando Cardinal Cento.

The two Secretariats were:

1. Secretariat on Modern Media of Communication (press, radio, theater, television, etc.), headed by Archbishop Martin J. O'Connor.
2. Secretariat for Promoting Christian Unity, headed by Augustin Cardinal Bea.

APPENDIX II

LIST OF ACTS AND DOCUMENTS
OF THE ANTEPREPARATORY COMMISSION

The Antepreparatory Commission published on March 29, 1961, four volumes of acts and documents.

Volume 1 contained the *Acta* of Pope John XXIII. All the allocutions of Pope John from his historic document of January 25, 1959, to his constitution of June 5, 1960, were contained in this 168-page volume.

Volume 2, in eight parts, contained the two thousand letters and documents of cardinals, patriarchs, bishops, vicars, and prefects apostolic, from every continent of the world.

Part I, Europe: 780 pages; 223 bishops: 16, Austria; 22, Belgium; 1, Denmark; 1, Finland; 109, France; 41, Germany; 30, Great Britain.

Part II, Europe: 810 pages; 228 letters of bishops: 1, Gibraltar; 5, Greece; 9, Holland; 1, Iceland; 30, Ireland; 1, Lithuania; 1, Luxembourg; 2, Malta; 1, Monaco; 2, Norway; 43, Poland; 23, Portugal; 82, Spain; 1, Sweden; 10, Switzerland; 3, Turkey; 12, Yugoslavia.

Part III, Italy: 942 pages; 311 letters from the Italian episcopacy.

Part IV, Asia: 662 pages; 229 letters from the Asiatic bishops: 2, Arabia; 1, Asiatic Turkey; 6, Burma; 1, Cambodia; 5, Ceylon; 55, China; 1, Cyprus; 1, Formosa; 63, India; 19, Indonesia; 4, Iran; 11, Iraq; 13, Japan; 1, Jordan; 5, Korea; 1, Laos;

35, Lebanon; 3, Malaysia; 8, Pakistan; 4, Palestine; 31, Philippines; 1, Rhodes; 24, Syria; 3, Thailand; 5, Vietnam.

Part V, Africa: 580 pages; 244 letters from the African hierarchy: 5, Algeria; 5, Angola; 4, Cameroons; 1, Cape Verde Islands; 9, Central West Africa; 35, Congo; 12, Egypt; 2, Eritrea; 3, Ethiopia; 1, Gambia; 5, Ghana; 3, Guinea; 1, Island of Réunion; 1, Mauritius; 8, Kenya; 1, Liberia; 3, Libya; 18, Madagascar; 2, Morocco; 6, Mozambique; 14, Nigeria; 4, Nyasaland; 10, Rhodesia; 5, Ruanda-Urundi; 1, Seychelles Islands; 2, Sierra Leone; 2, Somalia; 5, Sudan; 16, Tanganyika; 1, Togo; 1, Tunisia; 7, Uganda; 25, Union of South Africa, Basutoland, Swaziland; 22, West Africa.

Part VI, North and Central America: 694 pages; 348 letters from the hierarchy: 1, Bahamas; 6, British Caribbean Federation; 1, British Honduras; 60, Canada; 4, Costa Rica; 3, Cuba; 1, Curaçao Isle; 6, Dominican Republic; 3, Guadalupe, Martinique; 12, Guatemala; 7, Haiti; 5, Honduras; 72, Mexico; 6, Nicaragua; 4, Panama; 2, Puerto Rico; 6, San Salvador; 149, United States.

Part VII, South America and Oceania: 358 letters from the bishops: 33, Argentina; 14, Bolivia; 132, Brazil; 20, Chile; 35, Colombia; 17, Ecuador; 3, Guiana; 6, Paraguay; 28, Peru; 5, Uruguay; 17, Venezuela.

30, Australia; 1, Malaya; 3, Micronesia; 5, New Guinea and Archipelago of Bismark; 3, New Zealand; 6, Polynesia.

Part VIII, 109 letters with counsels and suggestions from superiors and generals of religious orders and institutes for youth education, for the apostolate among the working class, for charitable works or the missions, for clergy, and for diocesan-parish cooperation.

Volume 3 contained 412 pages of propositions and directives from the ten Sacred Congregations of the Roman Curia: Holy Office, Consistory, Oriental Church, Sacraments, Council, Religious, Propagation of the Faith, Rites, Extraordinary Ecclesiastical Affairs, and Seminaries and Universities.

Volume 4 contained the reports of Catholic and ecclesiastical universities from Rome and the world.

Part I, 562 pages from the Gregorian and Latin universities and *De Propaganda fidei*.

Part II, 460 pages from the universities in Rome: Angelicum, Athenaeum of St. Anselm, Anthonianium, Salesianum, Institute of Sacred Music, Institute of Christian Archaeology, Theological Faculty of St. Bonaventure, International College of Discalced Carmelites, and Marianum.

Part III, 824 pages from the 37 universities outside Rome.

APPENDIX III

THE CENTRAL PREPARATORY COMMISSION

In his *motu proprio, Superno Dei nutu* (*La Documentation Catholique*, June 19, 1960), Pope John stated: " The Central Commission has as its end the following and coordinating of the work of the various commissions. It will report their conclusions to us, so that we may be able to determine the subjects to be treated at the Ecumenical Council."

As of Nov. 7, 1961 (*La Documentation Catholique*, Feb. 19, 1961; Dec. 17, 1961), the Central Commission numbered 102 members and 29 counselors. There were 60 cardinals from 29 countries, 24 cardinals from the Roman Curia, and 36 residential bishops and archbishops from various countries.

The Members and Counselors of the Commission

PRESIDENT: His Holiness, Pope John XXIII
SECRETARY: His Excellency, Bishop Pericle Felici
MEMBERS: *Cardinals:* E. Tisserant, G. Pizzardo, B. Aloisi Masella, M. Mimmi, G. Cicognani, J. Van Roey, M. Gonçalves Cerejeira, A. Lienart, I. Tappouni, S. Copello, G. P. Agagianian, J. McGuigan, N. Gilroy, F. Spellman, T. De Gouveia, J. de Barros Camara, E. Pla y Deniel, M. Arteaga y Betancourt, J. Frings, A. Caggiano, T. Tienchensin, V. Valeri, P. Ciriaci,

C. M. de la Torre, G. Siri, J. d'Alton, J. McIntyre, S. Wyszynski, P. E. Leger, V. Gracias, F. Cento, A. Cicognani, J. Garibi y Rivera, A. M. Barbieri, W. Godfrey, F. Koenig, L. J. Muench, P. Tatsuo Doi, B. J. Alfrink, R. Santos, L. Rugambwa, A. Ottaviani, A. di Jorio, A. Jullien, A. Larraona, W. T. Heard, A. Bea, J. Doepfner, L. Concha Cordoba; these cardinals were later added: Micara, Traglia, Confalonieri, Quintero, Meyer, Testa, Roberti, Ferretto, Richaud, Quiroga y Palacios, Montini, Ruffini.

Patriarchs: Stephanos I Sidarouss (Alexandria — Copts), Maximos IV Saïgh (Antioch — Melkites), Paul Meouchi (Antioch — Maronites), Paul II Cheikho (Babylon — Chaldeans), A. Gori (Jerusalem — Latins).

Archbishops: A. Chacon (Merida), O. A. Beras (Santo Domingo), J. Ujcic (Belgrade), P. F. Ryan (Port of Spain), L. Chavez y Gonzalez (San Salvador), A. Silva Santiago (Concepcion), J. J. A. Mena Porta (Asuncion), J. Grosz (Kalocsa), A. I. Antezana y Rojas (La Paz), D. A. Campbell (Glasgow), T. B. Cooray (Colombo), P. T. McKeefry (Wellington), M. Lefevre (Dakar), K. J. Alter (Cincinnati), L. L. Graner (Dacca), D. E. Hurley (Durban), J. Landazuri Ricketts (Lima), P. Bernier (Gaspé), M. Perrin (Carthage), V. Bazin (Rangoon), F. Poirier (Port-au-Prince), M. Bernard (Brazzaville), J. Rakotomalala (Tananarive), B. Yago (Abidjan).

Residential Bishops: A. Verwimp (Kisantu), J. T. Suhr (Copenhagen), A. G. Jelmini (Thermai Basilicae and Apostolic Administrator of Lugano), P. M. Ngo-Dinh-Thuc (Saesina and Vicar Apostolic of Vinhlong).

Titular Bishops: L. I. Scharmach (Mostene and Vicar Apostolic of Rabaul), A. Soegijahranata (Danaba and Vicar Apostolic of Semarang), T. Quinlan (Furnot Major and Vicar Apostolic of Chunchon), M. J. O'Connor (President of Communications Secretariat).

These members were later added: Archbishops Seper and Bengsch, and Bishop Carpino.

Reverend Fathers: Dom Benno Gut (Prime Abbot of Benedictines), A. Sepinski (Minister General of Friars Minor), J. B. Janssens (General of Society of Jesus), M. Browne (General of Dominicans).

COUNSELORS: G. Cardinal Ferretto (Consistory).

Archbishops: G. Da Costa Nunes (Roman Church), P. Parente (Supreme Sacred Congregation of the Holy Office), P. Sigismondi (Sacred Congregation for the Propagation of the Faith), A. Samore (Sacred Congregation for Extraordinary Ecclesiastical Affairs), A. Dell'Acqua (Secretariat of State), E. Dante (Sacred Congregation of Rites), D. Staffa (Sacred Congregation of Seminaries and Universities), V. Bartoccetti (Supreme Tribunal of the Apostolic Signatura), F. Brennan (Sacred Roman Rota), P. Sfair, P. Pashini (Lateran University), S. Romani, C. Zerba (Sacred Congregation of the Sacraments), P. Palazzini (Sacred Congregation of the Council), P. Principi (Sacred Congregation of the Basilica of St. Peter).

Bishops: A. Wynen and A. Canestri (Sacred Roman Rota); A. Cavagna, G. Rossi (Sacred Apostolic Penitentiary); F. Tinello (Apostolic Chancery); M. Giusti (Vatican Archives).

Reverend Fathers: D. P. Salmon, O.S.B. (Abbot of St. Jerome of Rome), R. Garrigou-Lagrange, O.P., A. Vaccari, S.J., A. M. Albareda, O.S.B. (Vatican Library); A. Coussa (Basilian of Alep and Sacred Congregation for the Oriental Church); P. Philippe, O.P. (Sacred Congregation of Religious).

INDEXES

I. COMMISSIONS AND SCHEMATA

II. DOCUMENTS AND SOURCES USED

III. SUBJECTS

IV. PERSONS

NOTE: *Names in Appendix III are not included here.*